# THE ORNAMENTS OF THE MINISTERS
## AS SHOWN ON
## ENGLISH MONUMENTAL BRASSES

Alcuin Club Collections
XXII

# THE ORNAMENTS OF THE MINISTERS AS SHOWN ON ENGLISH MONUMENTAL BRASSES

BY

H. J. CLAYTON, A.K.C.

*Vicar of Bognor*

WIPF & STOCK · Eugene, Oregon

Wipf and Stock Publishers
199 W 8th Ave, Suite 3
Eugene, OR 97401

The Ornaments of the Ministers
as Shown on English Monumental Brasses
By Clayton, H. J.
Softcover ISBN-13: 978-1-6667-9433-5
Hardcover ISBN-13: 978-1-6667-9432-8
eBook ISBN-13: 978-1-6667-9434-2
Publication date 11/1/2021
Previously published by A. R. Mowbray & Co. Ltd., 1919

This edition is a scanned facsimile of
the original edition published in 1919.

# The Ornaments of the Ministers as shown on English Monumental Brasses

## INTRODUCTION

THE monumental brasses which lie on the floors of so many of our ancient parish churches do not profess to furnish us, except in rare and late examples, with portraits of the persons to whose memory they were made and laid down. They are, however, of considerable value as guides to the costumes worn by knights, civilians, judges, ladies, and ecclesiastics, from the latter part of the thirteenth century up to the end of the seventeenth century. They provide us with a sequence of examples of men in armour from 1277 to 1680; of civilian dress from about 1325 to 1685, with one late example dated 1773; of ladies' costume from 1310 to 1694. They show us also the dress of children and of widows. They illustrate academical costume and legal robes. They have much to teach in regard to heraldry. Their inscriptions are worthy of study for their lettering; while much can be learnt from the way in which the Persons of the Blessed Trinity and the Saints are represented.

We are concerned solely with the brasses which have been laid down to commemorate ecclesiastics, and of these some four hundred and fifty have survived the spoliation of the sixteenth and seventeenth centuries, the neglect of the eighteenth, and the process of "restoration" in the nineteenth. They provide us with an abundance of evidence for the interpretation of the Ornaments Rubric in the Book of Common Prayer so far as the ornaments of the ministers which were in use in the second year of the reign of Edward VI are concerned. They are, of course, part only of the evidence at our disposal. No wise person would attempt to reconstruct mediaeval armour solely from the study of monumental brasses;

but, on the other hand, he would be unwise if he totally neglected their evidence. In the same way one of the important links in the chain for the study of the Ornaments Rubric is provided by monumental brasses, though effigies, stained glass, portraits, illuminations, and the vestments which have survived, must also be considered in order that the whole of the evidence may be before us.

While the vestments remained the same from the fourteenth century (the earliest ecclesiastical brass being of the date *c.* 1311) to the issue of the Ornaments Rubric, a study of our brasses will show that there were changes in fashion. Not only is it the case that, in the absence of a dated inscription, we can fix, within narrow limits, the date of a brass by observing the manner in which the hair of the person commemorated is represented—for it is long and flowing, and curling behind the ears in the earliest examples, but gradually becomes less flowing till, by the Tudor period, it is usually quite straight—; but a study of the vestments which are worn will tell the same tale. In the earliest brasses they fit close to the figure, the drapery is well shown by means of deep and bold cutting, and there is an absence of shading, or at the least very little of it. The amice is at first loose and hanging low on the neck ; and the wrist apparels encircle the sleeves, whereas, in later times, they are represented by patches of embroidery only ; and the stole and maniple will, as a rule, be found to be widened at the ends.

As we are concerned only with those brasses which assist us in the illustration of the ornaments of the ministers as ordered in the Ornaments Rubric no attention need be paid to the representation of Pope St. Gregory the Great, in a triple tiara, on the brass representing the Mass of St. Gregory laid down to the memory of Roger Legh, 1506, and his wife Elizabeth, 1499, at Macclesfield ; to the small figure of St. Jerome vested as a cardinal, in the initial O of the inscription to Thomas Humfre, *c.* 1500, on a palimpsest brass at Great Berkhampsted ; to the small figure of St. Peter in triple tiara, holding a key and cross staff in his hands, and vested in crossed stole and cope, on the brass to Ralph, Lord Cromwell, *c.* 1470, at Tattershall. We may also pass over the brasses which commemorate priors, such as Thomas Nelond, 1433, at Cowfold; monks, like the series at St. Albans; nuns, such as Mary Gore, Prioress of Amesbury, 1436, at Nether Wallop; the friar on the palimpsest brass at Denham; and the abbess Elizabeth Harvey, with a broken pastoral staff, 1520, at Elstow.

With abbots, however, we are concerned, so far as they are shown dressed in the mass vestments of a bishop; while the brass of Abbot Richard Bewfforeste, *c.* 1510, at Dorchester (Fig. 75), and that of Nicholas of Louth, rector and builder of the chancel of Cottingham Church, 1383 (Fig. 74), have been included, as showing the choir habit of the Augustinian canons, especially the *cappa nigra*, or choral cope.

The earliest existing ecclesiastical brass is that of Richard de Hakebourne, *c.* 1311, in Merton College chapel (Fig. 17); though there was, till 1857, one which was probably earlier, viz. that to the memory of Adam de Bacon, *c.* 1310, at Oulton, Suffolk, from which church it was then stolen. Fortunately rubbings of it are in existence, and therefore it has been included (Fig. 16). The series of brasses of ecclesiastics continues after the issue of the Ornaments Rubric in 1559, and post-Reformation vestments can be studied in such examples as:—

> Leonard Hurst, 1560, in cassock, gown, and scarf, at Denham;
> William Dye, 1567, in cassock, surplice, and narrow scarf, at Westerham;
> Bishop Edmund Geste, 1578, in rochet, chimere, and scarf, in Salisbury Cathedral (Fig. 11);
> Bishop Robert Pursglove, 1579, in mass vestments, at Tideswell (Fig. 12);
> Bishop Henry Robinson, 1616, in rochet, chimere, and scarf, at Queen's College, Oxford (Fig. 13);
> Archbishop Samuel Harsnett, 1631, in cope and mitre, at Chigwell (Fig. 4).

The brasses of which illustrations are given may be divided into the following classes:—

1. Archbishops.
2. Bishops.
3. Mitred abbots.

## The Ornaments of the Ministers

4. Priests in mass vestments.
5. Priests in cope with almuce.
6. Priests wearing the almuce, but without the cope.
7. Priests in the choral cope (*cappa nigra*).
8. Figures of deacons in dalmatic.
9. Members of the Chapter of Windsor, wearing the mantle of the Order of the Garter.
10. Priests in surplice and scarf.

A few brasses, however, are exceptional, and cannot be placed in any of these divisions. For example, Edward Tacham, 1473, in Winchester College, is shown wearing surplice and cope, but has an amice where the almuce would be expected (Fig. 61); while in the palimpsest brass at St. Margaret's, Rochester, 1465, there is a double representation of Thomas Cod, who, in the one case, wears cope with amice, and in the other cope with almuce (Fig. 60). The almuce is probably also to be seen worn along with the mass vestments on the brasses of Bishop Thomas Goodryke, 1554, in Ely Cathedral (Fig. 10), and of Bishop Robert Pursglove, 1579, at Tideswell (Fig. 12).

In the brasses of Thomas Clerke, *c.* 1411, at Horsham (Fig. 44), and of John West, 1415, at Sudborough (Fig. 45), the figures are vested in amice, alb, crossed stole, and maniple, with the addition of the cope in the former instance. These two examples are of interest and importance, for they show that the maniple was, in England, worn in the procession before Mass, in distinction from the Roman custom of putting it on, with the chasuble, after the procession. Roger Hoveden speaks of a procession appointed "Cum sacerdote induto alba, et manipulo, et stola."[1] It is still so worn by the Dominicans; while De Moleon refers to its use in France at the beginning of the eighteenth century, for he tells us that at St. Maurice, Angers, "whenever the celebrant, deacon and subdeacon are in albs, whether for a procession or other ceremony, they always have the maniple."[2]

Certain broad conclusions may be stated in regard to the evidence furnished by English monumental brasses. The

---

[1] See Maskell, *Mon Rit*. III. 367 (edit. 1847).
[2] *Voyages Liturgiques*, edit. 1718, p 90.

alb is generally apparelled, both on the skirts and on the sleeves, and from the latter half of the fourteenth century the sleeve apparels are represented by patches instead of by embroidery entirely encircling the wrists. The amice is apparelled, though occasionally no embroidery is visible, and in some cases the chasuble is so worn as to hide part of the amice apparel. In early examples it is loose and hangs low on the neck, but later on it is more collar-like. The stole is long and narrow, and is usually embroidered over all that part of it which is visible below the chasuble. At times, especially in the earlier examples, it has expanding or squared ends. Where the whole of it is shown, as in the brasses of Thomas Clerke, c. 1411, at Horsham (Fig. 44), and of John West, 1415, at Sudborough (Fig. 45), it is embroidered throughout its whole length. The maniple too, like the stole, is, as a rule, embroidered throughout, and it, too, sometimes has expanding or squared ends.

The chasuble is shown on brasses as of the full Gothic shape, and folded back at the wrists. In the majority of examples it is represented as of quite plain material, its richness depending on its fullness and on its border ornament and orphrey. In the brasses of Bishop Richard Bell, 1496, in Carlisle Cathedral (Fig. 8) and of Laurence de Wardeboys, Abbot of Ramsey from 1508 to 1539, at Burwell (Fig. 15), the chasuble is of richly figured material. The border ornament on brasses consists either of a line, or series of lines, which may represent braid, or else of an elaborate decorated pattern. The orphrey in the earliest examples is of the Y or Ψ shape, but tends later on to be of the pillar type.

The illustrations of existing mediaeval chasubles given in the Victoria and Albert Museum Catalogue of " English Ecclesiastical Embroideries" show that vestments were constantly made of richly figured material, but in the majority of brasses the chasuble is represented as being made of plain material. In so frequently omitting the orphrey the brass-engravers were true to facts, for Dr. Wickham Legg has pointed out that "if we may trust the monuments of the Middle Ages that have come down to us, a large proportion of the mediaeval chasubles, especially in England, had no orphrey whatever"; and that "the absence of orphreys in the chasuble was very noticeable in the exhibition of mediaeval pictures that was got together by the Society of Antiquaries at Burlington House in the summer of 1896."[1] The engravers are also accurate in their use of the pillar orphrey, for it was actually so worn, with a Latin cross at the back. This, says the writer of the Victoria and Albert Museum Catalogue of "English Ecclesiastical Embroideries" was "the normal form of the back orphrey of the chasuble";[2] while Becon can be called as a witness to the same fact, for in *The Displaying of the Popish Mass* he speaks of chasubles on which there is "nothing at all but a cross upon the back to fray away spirits."

Heraldic and personal devices on chasubles are rare. The arms of Salisbury diocese are depicted on the pillar orphrey of John de Waltham, Bishop of Salisbury, 1395, in Westminster Abbey (Fig. 6); while on the chasuble of John Baker in the Fitzalan chapel at Arundel, 1445, are his initials, I. B., arranged as $\frac{I}{B}$ (Fig. 33). Mr. Druitt, in Appendix C of his *Costume on Brasses*, gives a list of chasubles with personal devices shown at the exhibition of the Burlington Fine Arts Club in 1905.

Mention may be made here of a few peculiarities on brasses, such as the omission of the stole (see Fig. 30); and of the maniple being placed on the right instead of on the left arm, on the brass of John Erton, 1503, at Newnton. This latter has not been illustrated, as it is most probably nothing but an error on the part of the engraver, though it must be remembered that the custom was not unknown, for the maniple was so worn by Carthusian consecrated nuns.

Archbishops, bishops, and abbots are shown in the mass vestments of a priest, with certain additions. The dalmatic is worn under the chasuble, and the tunicle under the dalmatic. The tunicle is normally plain and fringed, as is the dalmatic, though in a few examples the latter is represented as of a richly-embroidered material (see Figs. 9, 10, 15). In the brasses of Bishop John Trilleck, 1360, in Hereford Cathedral (Fig. 5), and of Bishop John de Waltham, 1395, in Westminster Abbey (Fig. 6), the tunicle is not shown, being either omitted or else the engraver may have

---

[1] *Transactions St. Paul's Ecclesiological Society*, vol. IV, p. 196 and n. 1.
[2] P. 5.

meant one to understand that it was of the same length as the dalmatic. In the brasses of Archbishop William de Grenefeld, 1315, in York Minster (Fig. 1); of Archbishop Robert de Waldeby, 1397, in Westminster Abbey (Fig. 2); of Archbishop Thomas Cranley, 1417, in New College, Oxford (Fig. 3); of Bishop John Trilleck, 1360, in Hereford Cathedral (Fig. 5); of Bishop Richard Bell, 1496, in Carlisle Cathedral (Fig. 8), the ornamented border of the sleeves of the dalmatic or tunicle can be seen round the right wrist.

In the brass of Bishop Thomas Goodryke, 1554, in Ely Cathedral (Fig. 10) the stole appears between the dalmatic and tunicle, instead of in its normal position underneath the latter.

The sandals are either covered with decoration or have stripes of embroidery on them ; and the episcopal gloves, at times with gauntlets hanging from the wrists and ending in a tassel, are embroidered, a jewel appearing on the back of the hand which holds the archiepiscopal cross or pastoral staff. The ring is on the middle finger of the right hand; but on the brass of Bishop Yong, 1526, at New College, Oxford (Fig. 9), rings are shown on all the fingers. Mr. Druitt draws attention to the vesting of the Abbot of Westminster for evensong, when " hys glovys and pontyfycales " are mentioned.[1] The mitre is sometimes plain, sometimes richly embroidered and jewelled, and sometimes crocketed ; while in some of the illustrations, especially in those of Bishop John Bowthe, 1478, at East Horsley (Fig. 7), and of Archbishop William de Grenefeld, 1315, in York Minster (Fig. 1), the *infulae* are plainly shown. They continued after the Reformation, as is shown on the brass of Archbishop Samuel Harsnett, 1631, at Chigwell (Fig. 4). At first the mitre is low, but grows taller, and in the latest examples has curved sides. The pastoral staff sometimes has the *vexillum* attached to it, as in the brass of Bishop John de Waltham, 1395, in Westminster Abbey (Fig. 6), and this too continues in the post-Reformation brass of Bishop Henry Robinson, 1616, at Queen's College, Oxford (Fig. 13). The pallium is worn by the archbishops who are commemorated on brasses, the number of crosses varying, there being ten on that of

---

[1] Op. cit., p. 74

## The Ornaments of the Ministers

William de Grenefeld (Fig. 1), six on that of Robert de Waldeby (Fig. 2), and seven on that of Thomas Cranley (Fig. 3). It is, naturally, not worn by Archbishop Samuel Harsnett (Fig. 4). At the present time the pallium worn by Roman Catholic archbishops (and certain bishops) is marked with six small black crosses, one on the breast and one on the back, one on each shoulder, and one on each pendant, though formerly the number varied, four being shown on the arms of the Sees of Canterbury and Dublin, five on those of Armagh.

The dalmatic is the special vestment of the deacon, but unfortunately there is no English brass to the memory of a deacon, with the exception of the mutilated palimpsest at Burwell, part of the reverse of which is made up of three pieces from an early, *c.* 1320, figure of a deacon, showing the dalmatic with its fringed border and orphreys, a portion of the maniple, the embroidered amice apparel, and the face. The lower part of the dalmatic can, however, be seen on the brasses of bishops and abbots; while, to compensate for the absence of brasses to deacons, there are the figures in which deacon saints are represented in that vestment. One of these has been reproduced, i.e. St. Stephen, on the brass of Laurence St. Maur, 1337, at Higham Ferrars (Fig. 77); while on the orphrey of the cope worn by William Ermyn, 1401, at Castle Ashby, St. Laurence is represented in alb, dalmatic, and maniple (see Fig. 49).

There are over one hundred brasses in which the figure is shown wearing a cope. This is often of plain material, but in several examples it is richly embroidered all over (see Figs. 52, 55, 58, 59). The hood is just visible on the cope worn by Bishop John White, *c.* 1548, in Winchester College (Fig. 59), and would appear to have been attached below the orphrey. The orphrey is generally narrow, even in the latest examples, and shows a considerable amount of variety in its ornamentation. The pattern is at times heraldic, as on the brass of Thomas Aileward, 1413, at Havant (Fig. 50); or it bears the initials of the person commemorated, as on the brass of John Mapilton, 1432, at Broadwater, where maple-leaves (as a rebus on his name) and the letter M (for his initial) appear (Fig. 53). There is an adaptation of the words of Job xix. 25, 26, on the brass of William Prestwyk, 1436, at Warbleton (Fig. 54). Saints under canopies, with tabernacle work, though not found on chasubles, save on that of Bishop John de Waltham, 1395, in Westminster Abbey (Fig. 6), are much more common on copes, and examples will be noticed on Figures 49, 52, and 56.

The morse partakes of the same diversity as the orphrey.

The fur almuce shows a certain amount of variety. Usually it is represented in the form of a hood with its cape, and with two long pendants hanging down in front; but on the brass of William Tanner, 1418, at Cobham, Kent, it is fastened in front with a brooch (Fig. 65); while on that of Ralph Elcok, 1510, at Tong, the cape portion is not so large as usual (Fig. 68). No pendants are shown on the brass of Robert Hacombleyn, 1528, at King's College, Cambridge (Fig. 70); and on the brasses of James Coorthopp, 1557, at Christ Church, Oxford (Fig. 71), and of Arthur Cole, 1558, at Magdalen College, Oxford (Fig. 80), the cape has been extended into a cloak, which in the latter example reaches to the knees. Attention must also be drawn to the brass of William de Rothewelle, 1361, at Rothwell (Fig. 46), where the hood of the almuce is plainly to be seen above the cope, and also the pendants hanging down in front; but of the cape there is no sign, though there is room enough left bare where the cope falls from the shoulders for it to be seen if it were there.[1] The brass of Matthew de Asscheton, 1400, at Shillington, may be compared with this (Fig. 48). There is no example on an English brass of the almuce being fastened with strings, as on the sculptured effigies of canons in Wells Cathedral.

The almuce is represented by means of white metal, engraved to represent fur; but in a few cases it is of incised brass, and probably represents the black fur almuce, as on the brasses of John de Campeden, 1382, at St. Cross, Winchester (Fig. 47), and of the priests in the choral copes (Figs. 72–75).

Was the almuce solely a choir vestment, or was it also worn with the mass vestments? It is impossible to give a definite answer if the evidence of brasses only is considered. Attention has already been drawn to the fact that

[1] See Dr Wickham Legg, op. cit, vol III, p. 43

it is, perhaps, worn by Bishops Thomas Goodryke (Fig. 10) and Robert Pursglove (Fig. 12). On sculptured tombs, however, it is shown with the mass vestments, and Sir William St. John Hope has drawn attention to the effigy attributed to Bishop Stanbury, who died in 1474, in Hereford Cathedral, where the grey almuce hangs out of the amice at the back of the neck; to the effigies of Bishop Goldwell at Norwich, of Bishop Wayneflete at Winchester, and of two priests, apparently members of the Chapter, in the north-east transept of the Cathedral Church of Wells.[1] This statement occurs as a footnote to Dr. Wickham Legg's paper on "The Black Scarf of Modern Church Dignitaries and the Grey Almuce of Mediaeval Canons," in the course of which he remarks that, "as a matter of fact, in England the grey almuce was worn under the mass vestments at the celebration of Mass. It would, of course, be completely hidden from view by the alb, and therefore the grey almuce can be but rarely detected in the representation of bishops and other dignitaries in their mass vestments."[2] He says it was "worn at mass at some of the more conservative churches in France, even to the end of the seventeenth century,"[3] giving three references to De Moleon's *Voyages Liturgiques*, edit. 1718, in support of this (pp. 119, 123, 141). None of these passages, however, refer to the wearing of the almuce under the alb and the chasuble, but merely to its being carried on the arm during Mass. A better reference would be to De Moleon's description of the church of St. Maurice at Angers, where, he says, there is a chapel with a painting which shows "a procession of all the clergy of the cathedral church with their vestments and ornaments. The canons have the chasuble and the almuce above it, as at Rouen, in winter."[4] Even here there is no reference to its being worn during Mass, but only in procession, for when De Moleon proceeds to describe the customs at Rouen he says that when the ministers " have arrived at the foot of the altar, both in winter and in summer, they put them off."[5] There are effigies (of Walter Idel, c. 1468, Simon Dods, 1496, and an unknown fifteenth-century canon) in Aberdeen Cathedral showing the almuce worn over the mass vestments.

---

[1] *Transactions St Paul's Ecclesiological Society*, vol. III, p. 46, n 5
[2] Op. cit., vol III, p 46.    [3] ibid    [4] p. 6    [5] p. 363.

That it was worn under the chasuble during Mass is clear, for Dr. Wickham Legg also points out that "in the blank leaves left before an inventory of the vestry of Westminster Abbey taken in 1388, there are written in an early sixteenth-century hand, directions for the vesting of the Abbot of Westminster at High Mass: 'Fyrst the westerer shall lay lowest the chesebell. above that the dalmatykes and the dalmatyk with the longest slevys uppermost and the other nethermost then hys stole and hys fanane and hys gyrdyll. opon that his albe thereopon hys gray Ames above that hys Rochett and uppermost hys kerchur with a vestry gyrdyll to tukk up his cole.'"[1] This makes it evident that the almuce was worn in the manner shown on the brasses mentioned, though it does not so occur on the only brass there is of an Abbot of Westminster, John Estney, 1498 (Fig. 14).

The evidence of mediaeval illuminations is clear. In the Pontifical known as the British Museum MS. Lansdowne 451 there are pictures of a bishop enclosing relics, and vested in alb, dalmatic, almuce, amice, cope, and mitre; of a bishop reconciling a church and in the same vestments; of a bishop blessing pontifical ornaments, and in the same vestments; and also of a bishop giving the episcopal benediction, and represented as wearing alb, dalmatic, almuce, amice, chasuble, mitre, and gloves. The hood of the almuce is plainly to be seen, as the figure is turned somewhat sideways.[2]

The almuce is not always worn with the surplice and cope, for on the brasses of John Lovelle, 1438, at St. George's, Canterbury (Fig. 62); of William Kirkeby, 1458, at Theydon Gernon (Fig. 63); and of an unknown priest, *c.* 1460, in the Temple Church, Bristol (Fig. 64), it is omitted.

At times its place is taken by the apparelled amice. Edward Tacham, 1473, in Winchester College chapel

---

[1] Op. cit., III, 46

[2] See Frere, *Pontifical Services*, Alcuin Club Collections IV, plate xi, figures 33–36. At Sarum it was sometimes worn under the chasuble, for Chancellor C. Wordsworth quotes the Salisbury Cathedral Statutes as allowing dignitaries and canons "when there is danger of taking cold while celebrating, 'sub *amictu* lineo *almuciis* suis libere, cum voluerint uti,' to protect their throats."—*Notes on Mediaeval Services*, p. 107, n. 1

## The Ornaments of the Ministers

(Fig. 61), is represented as vested in surplice, cope, and amice (as is Richard North, 1445, in the same place); while the palimpsest brass of Thomas Cod, 1465, in St. Margaret's Church, Rochester (Fig. 60), shows on the one side a figure vested in surplice, cope, and almuce; and on the other the same person vested in surplice, cope, and apparelled amice. According to the modern Roman Pontifical the bishop, when administering Confirmation, is to be vested in a rochet, or if he be a regular, in a surplice, with amice, stole, white cope, and mitre; and it is possible that the custom of wearing the amice with the surplice was not unknown in England in mediaeval days.

The *cappa nigra*, or black choral cope, is shown on the brasses of an unknown priest, *c.* 1370, at Watton (Fig. 72); of Adam Ertham, 1382, in the Fitzalan chapel at Arundel (Fig. 73); of Nicholas of Louth, 1383, at Cottingham (Fig. 74); and probably in that of Richard Bewfforeste, *c.* 1510, at Dorchester, Oxon. (Fig. 75). Mr. Cuthbert Atchley describes it as "a black cloth cope or cloak worn over amess and surplice, open in front, reaching to the heels. It was worn by all ranks in choir during the winter months, generally from October or November to Easter, at all services, except when silk copes were prescribed; all the year round at mattins, at which service more protection from cold was needed, because of its early hour. In most instances there was a hood attached to the back of the cloak."[1] In the first year of the reign of Edward VI it was forbidden everywhere "because it is thought to be a kind of monkery."[2]

From the evidence furnished by brasses it would appear that the choral cope was put on over the head, as none of the illustrations show a fastening at the neck, though if the cope worn by William de Rothewelle, *c.* 1361, at Rothwell (Fig. 46) be, as Mr. Druitt says, a slightly-ornamented form of the choral cope, it is there fastened at the neck by a brooch. It is, perhaps, worth notice that around the tomb of Thomas and Beatrix Fitzalan in the Fitzalan chapel at Arundel, there are twenty-eight figures of priests wear-

---

[1] *Transactions St Paul's Ecclesiological Society*, vol iv, pp. 317, 318.
[2] See Frere, *Visitation Articles and Injunctions* (Alcuin Club Collections), vol. xv, pp. 149, 153, 161.

ing the choral cope; but in the case of one only (the centre figure facing west) is the cope closed. In the other twenty-seven examples it is fastened at the neck by a morse of varying shape.

There are three brasses showing members of the Chapter of Windsor in the mantle of the Order of the Garter, with a circular badge on the left shoulder, bearing (argent) a cross (gules) :—

Roger Parkers, *c.* 1370, North Stoke (Fig. 78).
Roger Lupton, 1540, Eton College chapel (Fig. 79).
Arthur Cole, 1558, Magdalen College, Oxford (Fig. 80).

In the brasses of Roger Parkers and of Arthur Cole the mantle is fastened with cords, while in that of Roger Lupton the fastening is by means of a small morse.

Many of the illustrations of priests in surplice and cope will show that there are two garments worn under the surplice. These are sometimes described as an undergarment and a cassock, but in the description of the illustrations they are spoken of as a cassock and a gown or pelisse. The so-called under-garment is the cassock, and has tight sleeves which at times extend over part of the hands like mittens. The upper-garment is the gown or pelisse worn over the cassock, the surplice (*superpelliceum*) being put on over this. In the earliest examples this gown has close sleeves, no wider than those of a modern cassock, but in the later ones the sleeves are wider, and are frequently edged or lined with fur. The brass of William Lawnder, *c.* 1530, at Northleach (Fig. 76), will show plainly the cassock under the wide fur sleeves of the gown, and over this the surplice.

The surplice is invariably long and gathered. In many cases it reaches to, or even covers, the feet, while in the shortest examples it extends to between the knees and the feet (see the brass of Richard Adams, 1522, at East Malling, Fig. 69).

The tippet, or scarf, is shown on the brass of William Lawnder, *c.* 1530, at Northleach (Fig. 76), as fastened on the left shoulder by a brooch, and as coming round behind the figure on to the right shoulder. On the brasses of Bishop Edmund Geste, 1578, in Salisbury Cathedral (Fig. 11), and of Henry Robinson, 1616, at Queen's College, Oxford (Fig. 13), it is a long scarf.

The Flemish brasses of Abbot Delamare, c. 1375, in St. Albans Abbey (Fig. 83), of Simon de Wenslagh, c. 1360, at Wensley (Fig. 81), and of (?) Thomas de Horton, c. 1360, at North Mimms (Fig. 82), have been included, though, strictly speaking, they represent continental rather than English vestments. The only point in connection with them on which comment is necessary is that the apparel of the amice is, in each example, long, and lying low on the neck, as in English brasses of the same period ; though, as is pointed out by Dr. Dearmer in *Dat Boexken vander Missen*, the Low Country custom, at all events in the period immediately before the Reformation, was to represent the apparel as very short.[1]

Figures of ecclesiastics in academic dress have been omitted, partly because they do not represent the ornaments of the ministers at the times of their ministrations, and partly in the hope that this subject will be dealt with by a competent authority in a separate volume. In the meanwhile reference may be made to Professor E. C. Clark's paper in the *Archaeological Journal* for 1893 (vol. l); to Mr. Atchley's paper, " The Hood as an Ornament of the Minister at the time of his Ministration in Quire and elsewhere" in vol. iv of the *Transactions of the St. Paul's Ecclesiological Society*, and to chapter ii of Mr. Druitt's *Costume on Brasses*.

It remains to thank those who have helped in the preparation of this book. Mr. F. C. Eeles and Mr. Mill Stephenson have given the writer much assistance, and the latter has lent several blocks belonging to the (late) Monumental Brass Society and to himself. The Oxford Press has allowed the use of blocks from the journal of the (late) Oxford University Brass Rubbing Society, and of one block from Dr. Dearmer's *Parson's Handbook*. Mr. Miller Christy and Dr. Bertram Smith have lent blocks of some Essex brasses, and their kindness is the greater in view of the fact that these illustrations will appear in their projected volume on the brasses of that county ; Mr. Cecil Davis has lent a block of a Bristol brass, and Mr. C. J. P. Cave blocks of Winchester brasses;

---

[1] *Alcuin Club Collections*, vol. v, p. 13

while rubbings and photographs of brasses have been supplied by the Victoria and Albert Museum, Mr. W. E. Gawthorp, the Rev. W. Marshall, and the Rev. R. W. M. Lewis ; and Messrs. Mowbray & Co. have allowed the use of the blocks of William de Rothewelle from the *English Churchman's Kalendar* for 1918, and of Bishop Edmund Geste from Dr. Dearmer's *Ornaments of the Ministers*.

Dr. Brightman has kindly read both the MS. and the proofs, making many most useful suggestions which the writer has gladly incorporated, and at the same time saving him from many errors.

# WILLIAM DE GRENEFELD,

*Archbishop of York, and Lord Chancellor.* 1315.

YORK MINSTER, YORKSHIRE.

THE mutilated effigy of an archbishop in mass vestments. Some eighteen inches out of a total length of sixty-eight inches have been lost, having been stolen by workmen about the year 1829.

The mitre is low and jewelled, and the *infulae* are plainly visible. These are marked with crosses.

The amice is apparelled and lies low on the neck.

The chasuble is represented as of plain material, with an ornamented border; and over it is worn the pallium, which is marked with ten crosses.

The right hand, two fingers of which are missing, is raised in blessing. Round the right wrist is the ornamented border of the sleeve of the dalmatic or tunicle.

On the left arm is worn the maniple, which has the unusual decoration of a series of seven crosses. The left hand is gloved, a jewel being shown on the back. This hand holds the staff of a pastoral staff or of an archiepiscopal cross, the head of which is lost.

A portion only of the dalmatic is visible.

Figure 1

William de Grenefeld. 1315. York Minster.

# ROBERT DE WALDEBY,

*Archbishop of York.* 1397.

**WESTMINSTER ABBEY.**

THE effigy of an archbishop in mass vestments.

The mitre is jewelled, and the *infulae* are not visible.

The amice is apparelled, as is the skirt of the alb.

The chasuble is of plain material and without either orphrey or border ornament. Over it is worn the pallium, which is marked with six crosses.

Under the chasuble is the dalmatic, which is of plain material, and fringed both at the bottom and the sides; and under this the unfringed tunicle, which also is plain save for a double line, probably representing braid. The ends of the embroidered stole appear below the tunicle.

The sandals are embroidered with stripes.

The right hand is raised in blessing, the thumb and first two fingers being extended, and on the middle finger is a ring. Round the right wrist is the ornamented border of the sleeve of the dalmatic or tunicle.

On the left hand is a glove with jewel; on the arm is the maniple, which is embroidered its whole length, and this hand grasps an archiepiscopal cross.

Waldeby was successively Bishop of Ayre in Aquitaine, Archbishop of Dublin, Bishop of Chichester, and Archbishop of York; and was tutor to Edward the Black Prince.

Figure 2

Robert de Waldeby.   1397.   Westminster Abbey.

# THOMAS CRANLEY,

*Archbishop of Dublin and Warden of New College.* 1417.

### NEW COLLEGE, OXFORD.

The effigy of an archbishop in mass vestments.

The mitre is jewelled, the *infulae* not showing.

The amice is apparelled, as is the skirt of the alb.

The chasuble is of plain material, without an orphrey; but it has as a border ornament a series of lines. Over it is worn the pallium, which is marked with seven crosses.

The dalmatic and tunicle are both plain and fringed, the stole appearing below the latter.

The sandals have a broad band of ornament.

The right hand is raised in blessing, and there is a ring on the middle finger; and the ornamented border of the sleeve of the dalmatic or tunicle can be seen round the right wrist.

On the left hand is a jewelled glove. The maniple, embroidered its whole length, is on the left arm, and the left hand grasps an archiepiscopal cross, part of which has been lost.

Thomas Cranley. 1417.
New College, Oxford.

# SAMUEL HARSNETT,

*Archbishop of York.* 1631.

### CHIGWELL, ESSEX.

The effigy of a post-Reformation archbishop, laid down in accordance with his will, dated February 13, 1630-31, in which he ordered :—

"My body I will to be buried within the Parrishe churche of Chigwell, withoute pompe or solempnitye at the foote of Thomazine late my beloved wief havinge only a Marble stone layde uppon my Grave w$^{th}$ a Plate of Brasse moulten into the Stone an ynche thicke haveinge the effigies of a Bysshope stamped uppon it w$^{th}$ his Myter and Crosiers staffe but the Brasse to be so rivited & fastened cleane throughe the Stone as sacrilegious handes maye not rend off the one w$^{thoute}$ breakinge the other."

He wears a high mitre, the *infulae* of which are visible ; ruff ; long rochet, which is ornamented at the neck and lower border ; chimere ; and cope.

The morse of the cope is hidden by the archbishop's beard. The cope is embroidered all over, and has a narrow orphrey.

His right hand presses a book to his breast, while he holds his pastoral staff, in the crook of which there is a rose, in his left hand.

There is no *vexillum* ; no gloves ; and no episcopal ring.

There are four shields of arms, Harsnett, and Harsnett impaling the Sees of Chichester, Norwich, and York.

Below the effigy is the inscription :—

" Qvod ipsissimvm Epitaphivm ex abvndanti
hvmilitate sibi poni Testamento cvravit
Reverendissimvs Praesvl."

The fillet inscription, which has the evangelistic symbols in the four corners, reads :—

" Hic iacet Samvell Harsnett qvondam vicarivs hvivs Ecclesiæ primo Indignvs Episcopvs Cicestriensis De[inde]- indignior Episcop' Norwicencis : Demvm Indignissim' Archiepiscop' Eboracēn : qvi obijt xxv die Maij Anno Dn̄i : 1631."

Figure 4

Samuel Harsnett. 1631. Chigwell.

# JOHN TRILLECK,

*Bishop of Hereford.* 1360.

HEREFORD CATHEDRAL, HEREFORDSHIRE.

The effigy of a bishop in mass vestments.

The mitre is jewelled, the *infulae* not being shown.

The amice is apparelled, as is the skirt of the alb.

The chasuble is of plain material, and without orphrey, having lines for border ornament.

The dalmatic is plain, and fringed on the sides, and on its lower edge. The tunicle is not shown in this example. The ends of the stole appear below the dalmatic.

The right hand is raised in blessing. There is a ring on the middle finger; and round the wrist is the ornamented border of the sleeve of the dalmatic.

The maniple, which is embroidered its whole length, is on the left arm, and in the left hand is the pastoral staff, which is without the *vexillum*.

The sandals have no embroidery.

Figure 5

JOHN TRILLECK.   1360.   HEREFORD CATHEDRAL.

# JOHN DE WALTHAM,

*Bishop of Salisbury and Lord High Treasurer.* 1395.

### WESTMINSTER ABBEY.

THE mutilated effigy of a bishop in mass vestments, the missing part of the figure, which "was stolen at the last (Queen Victoria's) Coronation," being taken from Moule and Harding's *Westminster Abbey*, 1825.

The mitre is plain and crocketed, the *infulae* not showing.

The amice is apparelled, as is the skirt of the alb, but no apparel is visible at the wrists.

The chasuble is of plain material, with a slight border ornament, and with a pillar orphrey ornamented with crosses alternating with the figure of the Blessed Virgin Mary holding our Lord on one arm, and with a sceptre in the other—the arms of the See of Salisbury. The dalmatic is of plain material, and fringed at the sides and bottom. The tunicle is not worn. The stole appears below the dalmatic. The sandals are embroidered with stripes.

The right hand is raised in blessing, and there is a ring on the middle finger.

On the left arm is a long narrow maniple embroidered its whole length; and the left hand holds a pastoral staff (the head of which is lost) with the *vexillum* attached to it.

Figure 6

JOHN DE WALTHAM. 1395. WESTMINSTER ABBEY.

# JOHN BOWTHE,

*Bishop of Exeter.* 1478.

### EAST HORSLEY, SURREY.

The kneeling effigy of a bishop in profile, in mass vestments.

The pastoral staff is held between the body and the left arm.

The mitre is jewelled, and shows the *infulae* or ornamented and fringed strips of silk embroidery hanging from the back.

The amice is apparelled, but there is no apparel on the skirt of the alb.

The chasuble is decorated with a pillar orphrey and an ornamented border.

The dalmatic is worn below the chasuble, but the tunicle is not shown.

The inscription is in black letter :—

" Quisquis eris qui transieris sta plege plora
Sum q$^d$ eris fuerā qe q$^d$es : pro me precor ora.
Hic iacet Johēs bowthe quōdā Ep̄s Exoniēn qui
Obiit v° die mēsis Aprelis A° dn̄i M° cccc° LXX°VIIJ°."

The arms are [argent] three boars' heads erect and erased [sable], a label of three points [gules] for difference.

Figure 7

JOHN BOWTHE. 1478. EAST HORSLEY.

# RICHARD BELL,

*Bishop of Carlisle.* 1496.

CARLISLE CATHEDRAL, CUMBERLAND.

THE effigy of a bishop in mass vestments.

He wears a high jewelled and crocketed mitre, the *infulae* of which are not visible.

The amice is apparelled, as is the skirt of the alb.

The chasuble is of a richly-figured material, with an ornamented border and a plain pillar orphrey.

The dalmatic is of plain material, and is not fringed, but has an ornamented border. The tunicle is of plain material and fringed. The stole appears below the tunicle.

The sandals have stripes of embroidery on them.

The right hand is gloved, with a jewel on the back, and holds a book on which is inscribed " Haec spes mea in sinu meo." Round the right wrist is the ornamented border of the sleeve of the dalmatic or tunicle.

On the left arm is the maniple, which is embroidered its whole length ; and the left hand grasps a pastoral staff, to which the *vexillum* is attached.

Figure 8

RICHARD BELL. 1496. CARLISLE CATHEDRAL.

# JOHN YONG,

## Bishop of Callipolis. ob. 1526.

**NEW COLLEGE, OXFORD.**

The mutilated effigy of a bishop in mass vestments, the head, and the top of the pastoral staff having been lost.

He wears sandals which are ornamented with stripes ; alb, which is not apparelled ; stole ; plain fringed tunicle ; dalmatic, which is fringed and of figured material ; and chasuble, which has an ornamented border and a pillar orphrey.

The right hand is raised in blessing. The thumb and first two fingers are raised, and rings are shown on the thumb and all the fingers.

The left hand holds a pastoral staff to which the *vexillum* is attached.

The maniple is omitted.

The gloves are loose round the wrists and are tasselled.

The inscription is in black letter :—

"Orate pro aīa Johīs yong Calipoleñ Epī
et custodis hui' Collegij qui obiit Anno dñi millmō
ccccc . . . die vero mensis. . . .
Cuius Anime propicietur deus. Amen."

The matrix shows the mitre to have been crocketed.

The incomplete inscription shows that the brass was made during the bishop's lifetime.

JOHN YONG. *ob.* 1526. NEW COLLEGE, OXFORD.

# THOMAS GOODRYKE,

*Bishop of Ely and Lord High Chancellor.* 1554.

ELY CATHEDRAL, CAMBRIDGESHIRE.

THE effigy of a bishop in mass vestments.

The mitre is jewelled, the *infulae* not being visible.

The amice is apparelled, as is also the skirt of the alb.

The chasuble is of plain material, with an ornamented border and an embroidered pillar orphrey.

The dalmatic is of a figured material, and is fringed at the bottom and sides; while the tunicle, which also is fringed, is of plain material. The stole is shown as between the dalmatic and the tunicle.

In his right hand, from which hangs the tassel of a glove, is a book with a seal attached.

On the left wrist is the maniple, embroidered its whole length; while the left hand, from which hangs the tassel of a glove, holds a pastoral staff with the *vexillum* attached to it.

The sandals are embroidered.

The almuce appears to be worn in this example under the mass vestments, part of it showing round the neck above the amice.

Figure 10

Thomas Goodryke. 1554. Ely Cathedral.

# EDMUND GESTE,

*Bishop of Salisbury.* 1578.

SALISBURY CATHEDRAL, WILTSHIRE.

THE effigy of a post-Reformation bishop.

He may be represented as wearing gown; rochet, which is buttoned at the neck; chimere; and scarf.

It is, however, possible that he is represented as wearing a gown over a cassock, or else a doctor's habit over gown and cassock.

He holds a book in his left hand, and in his right the ornamented hilt of a pommelled walking-staff with pointed foot.

Figure 11

EDMUND GESTE. 1578. SALISBURY CATHEDRAL.

# ROBERT PURSGLOVE,

*Suffragan Bishop of Hull.* 1579.

TIDESWELL, DERBYSHIRE.

THE effigy of a bishop in mass vestments. In using this as a post-Reformation example of the vestments ordered by the Ornaments Rubric it must be borne in mind that Bishop Pursglove refused to take the Oath of Supremacy to Elizabeth in 1559, and resigned. He was described as "stiff in papistry."

He wears a low mitre, which is jewelled.

The amice is apparelled, as is the skirt of the alb.

The chasuble is of plain material, with an embroidered pillar orphrey and ornamented border.

The dalmatic is plain and fringed, and below this is the fringe of the tunicle; the ends of the stole appearing below the latter.

The sandals are ornamented.

The hands are joined in prayer, and on them are gloves, with a jewel showing on the back of the right hand, and gloves with tassels hang from the wrists.

There is no maniple on the left arm.

The pastoral staff, without the *vexillum*, lies across the left part of the body.

As in the brass of Bishop Goodryke (Fig. 10), the almuce appears to be shown round the neck, worn below the vestments.

Figure 12

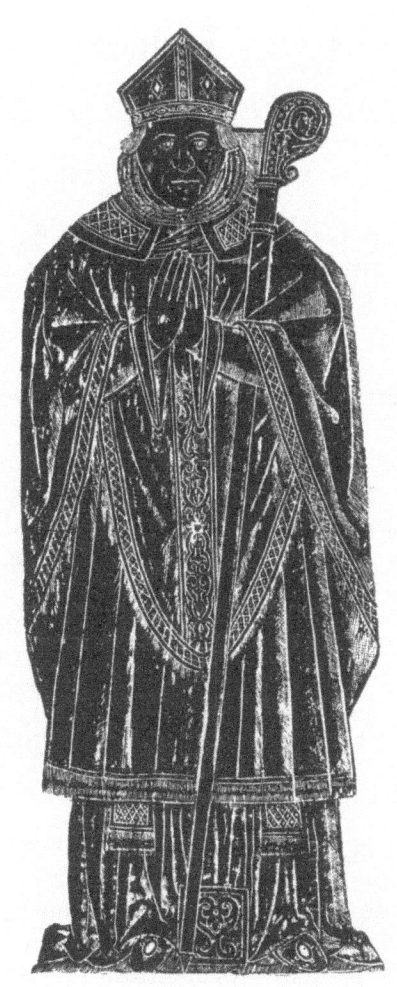

Robert Pursglove. 1579. Tideswell.

# HENRY ROBINSON,

*Bishop of Carlisle and Provost of Queen's College.* 1616.

QUEEN'S COLLEGE, OXFORD.

A RECTANGULAR plate containing the effigy of a bishop kneeling on a cushion, and wearing his out-of-door dress.

His gown can be seen at the neck, and he wears rochet, chimere, and scarf. Round the neck and wrists are ruffs.

The chimere is open, and turned back with lapels; the rochet has full sleeves, and is embroidered at the neck. The scarf is long and full. On the head is a skull cap.

The lower part of the pastoral staff bears the inscription "*Ps.* 23. *Corrigendo.*" The middle part is twisted, and is inscribed "SVSTENTANDO." At the upper end is an angel supporting the crook, which is decorated with round knobs, on the topmost of which is a crane holding a stone in its claw. In the middle of the crook is an eye, and round the crook are the words "*Vigilando*" and "*Dirigendo.*" Hanging from the crook is the *vexillum*, which is inscribed "*Velando.*" In the right hand of the bishop is a lighted candle, and on its halo the words "'Επιφάναι τοῖς ἐν σκότει. Lu. 1."

In the background is a representation of Carlisle Cathedral, in the doorway of which three bishops, similarly vested, appear to be ordaining a kneeling figure wearing a gown with "false" sleeves; and of Queen's College, with three graduates in their "formalities."

Henry Robinson. 1616. Queen's College, Oxford

# JOHN ESTNEY,

*Abbot of Westminster.* 1498.

WESTMINSTER ABBEY.

THE effigy of an abbot of Westminster in mass vestments. Attention is drawn in the Introduction to the almuce being worn with the mass vestments by the abbots of Westminster, but in this example it is not shown.

On the head is a richly-embroidered and jewelled mitre, part of the *infulae* being shown.

The amice is apparelled, as in the skirt of the alb.

The chasuble is of plain material, with border ornament and embroidered pillar orphrey.

The dalmatic is of plain material and fringed on the sides and bottom ; while the plain tunicle is unfringed, the stole appearing below it.

The sandals have two lines on them as ornament.

The right hand is raised in blessing, and there is a ring on the middle finger ; while the cuff of the glove is tasselled. The left hand holds a pastoral staff with the *vexillum* attached to it ; and from the left wrist hangs the maniple, which is embroidered its whole length.

Close to the head is a scroll, bearing in black letter, " Exultabo in deo Ihū meo."

Figure 14

JOHN ESTNEY.   1498.   WESTMINSTER ABBEY.

# LAURENCE DE WARDEBOYS.

*Died,* 1542.

BURWELL, CAMBRIDGESHIRE.

The lower portion of the effigy of an abbot in mass vestments.

The chasuble is of a richly figured material, and has an embroidered pillar orphrey.

The dalmatic also is of figured material and is fringed at the bottom and on the sides.

The tunicle has an ornamented border.

Part of the stole appears below the tunicle; and part of the maniple can be seen hanging from the left wrist.

The lower part of the pastoral staff remains, the tassels of the *vexillum* showing on either side of the staff.

The alb is apparelled on the skirt.

Laurence de Wardeboys was Abbot of Ramsey from 1500 to 1539, and the brass was probably prepared before his death in 1542. By that time the abbey had been suppressed, and the brass was reversed, and engraved on the other side with a representation of the abbot in gown, surplice, and almuce, with his head resting on a cushion.

Laurence de Wardeboys. *ob.* 1542. Burwell.

# ADAM DE BACON.

## *c.* 1310.

#### FORMERLY AT OULTON, SUFFOLK.

The effigy of a priest in mass vestments.

The amice is apparelled and hangs low on the neck.

The apparels on the sleeves of the alb entirely encircle the wrists. Its skirt also is apparelled, and the bottom part of the alb is represented as falling into folds not unlike those of the linen fold pattern in woodwork.

The chasuble is of plain material, with a border ornament, but without any orphrey.

The maniple is embroidered its whole length; as is also the part of the stole which is visible below the chasuble, both stole and maniple having slightly expanding ends.

This brass was stolen from Oulton church in February, 1857.

Figure 16

ADAM DE BACON.   c. 1310.
OULTON (FORMERLY AT).

# RICHARD DE HAKEBOURNE.

### *c.* 1311.

#### MERTON COLLEGE, OXFORD.

The half-length effigy of a bearded priest in mass vestments, and placed in the head of a floriated cross, nearly all of which has been lost.

The amice is apparelled, and embroidered with fylfots, etc. The apparels on the sleeves of the alb encircle the wrists.

The border of the plain chasuble is also embroidered.

Haines, *Manual of Monumental Brasses* (1861), p. cxlii, describes this brass as "evidently the work of the same artist as the fine effigy lately at Oulton" (see Fig. 16).

RICHARD DE HAKEBOURNE. c. 1311.
MERTON COLLEGE, OXFORD.

# THOMAS DE HOP.

### *c.* 1320.

##### KEMSING, KENT.

THE half-length effigy of a priest in mass vestments.

Two buttons of a cassock are to be seen on each wrist.

The amice is apparelled with fylfot and quatrefoil ornamentation, and hangs low on the neck.

There is an ornamented border to the plain chasuble; and the apparels on the sleeves of the alb encircle the wrists.

The inscription over the head of the figure is in black letter, and reads:—

"Hic iacet dominus Thomas de hop."

Figure 18

Thomas de Hop. c. 1320. Kemsing.

## AN UNKNOWN PRIEST.

### *c.* 1320.

#### STOKE-IN-TEIGNHEAD, DEVONSHIRE.

THE effigy of a priest in mass vestments.

The amice is apparelled, as is the alb, both on the skirt and on the sleeves. In this example these do not encircle the wrists as is often the case in brasses of the first half of the fourteenth century.

The maniple and stole are embroidered throughout, and have squared ends.

The chasuble is of plain material, and without orphrey or border ornament.

Anon. *c.* 1320. Stoke-in-Teignhead.

# NICHOL DE GORE.

## *c.* 1330.

#### WOODCHURCH, KENT.

The effigy of a priest in mass vestments in a quatrefoiled circle set in a floriated cross ; and bearing a French inscription in Lombardic characters. The execution of the figure is poor, the neck and hands being greatly out of proportion ; but the figure is noticeable for the Y-shaped orphrey of the chasuble, and the ornament which connects the arms of the Y.

The amice is apparelled, and the maniple is embroidered ; but the stole is not. The skirt of the alb also is apparelled, while the apparels on the sleeves of the amice encircle the wrists.

The inscription is :—

"✠ mestre : nichol : de : gore : gıst : en : ceste : place : ıhesu : crist : prioms : ore : qe : merci : luı : pace."

Figure 20

Nichol de Gore.   c. 1330.   Woodchurch.

## LAURENCE ST. MAUR.

### 1337.

#### HIGHAM FERRARS, NORTHAMPTONSHIRE.

THE effigy of a priest in mass vestments.

The amice is apparelled and hangs low on the neck.

The chasuble is of plain material and without orphrey, but with an ornamented border.

The sleeves and skirt of the alb are apparelled.

The maniple is partly hidden by the folds of the chasuble, but the part which is visible is embroidered. The stole, which has splayed ends, is long, and partly covers the apparel on the skirt of the alb.

The sleeves of the cassock are visible at the wrists.

Beneath the feet of the figure are two dogs quarrelling over a bone.

On the breast is a black letter inscription :—

"Fili dei miserere mei."

It is worth notice that the ornamentation on the apparels of the amice and alb, and on the stole, maniple, and border of the chasuble are not alike, each differing from the others.

Laurence St. Maur.　1337.　Higham Ferrars.

# HENRY DE GROFHURST.

*c.* 1340.

HORSEMONDEN, KENT.

THE effigy of a bearded priest in mass vestments, the feet resting on a lion.

The alb is apparelled on the skirt and on the sleeves, in the latter case the apparel encircling the wrists.

The amice is apparelled; and the maniple, which has expanding ends, is embroidered its whole length, both sides of it being shown.

The stole also has expanding ends which are ornamented with roses.

The chasuble has a Y-shaped orphrey and an ornamented border, and is cut to a right angle at the bottom.

An inscription in black letter is on a scroll across the breast. Cf. the brass of Laurence St. Maur at Higham Ferrars (Fig. 21) :—

"Qui dedit maneriū de leueshothe abbati & conventiu de beghāme ad inueniēdum unū ppetuū capellanū celebrantē ī ecclesia de horsmondñe & capella de leueshothe."

Some authorities consider this brass to be French work.

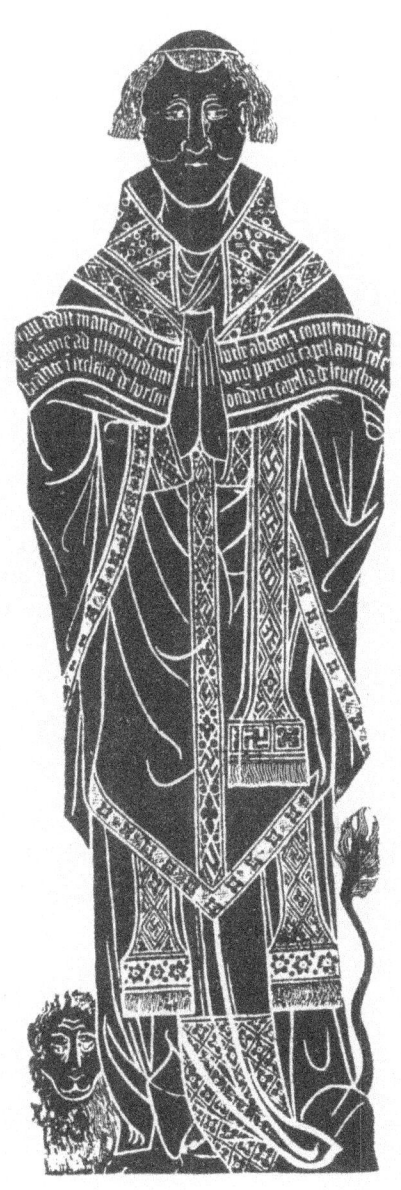

Henry de Grofhurst.   c. 1340.   Horsemonden.

# RICHARD DE BELTOUN.

### *c.* 1340.

#### CORRINGHAM, ESSEX.

The half-length effigy of a priest in mass vestments.

The apparel of the amice is large, and hangs low on the neck. The apparels on the sleeves of the alb encircle the wrists.

The chasuble is of plain material, without orphrey, but with an ornamented border.

The maniple hangs from the left arm, and is embroidered.

The inscription is in black letter :—

"Hic iacet dn̄s Ricardus de Beltōū qndā
Rector istius ecclīe cui' aīe ₚpicietur deus"

Figure 23

RICHARD DE BELTOUN. c. 1340. CORRINGHAM.

# AN UNKNOWN PRIEST.

## *c.* 1370.

#### SHOTTESBROOKE, BERKSHIRE.

The effigy of a priest in mass vestments.

The amice is apparelled. The sleeves of the cassock are visible at the wrists; and the sleeves of the alb are apparelled. There is a large apparel on the skirt of the alb.

The maniple is embroidered its whole length, and, like the stole, has squared ends.

The chasuble is of plain material, and without an orphrey, but has a double-line running as ornament round its border.

The ornamentation on the amice apparel, the alb apparels, the stole, and the maniple consists of fylfots and quatrefoils.

ANON. c. 1370. SHOTTESBROOKE.

# PETER DE LACY.

## 1375.

#### NORTHFLEET, KENT.

THE effigy of a priest in mass vestments. The fillet inscription (which has been omitted) describes him as Rector of Northfleet and Prebendary of Swerdes in the Cathedral of Dublin.

The amice is apparelled, as is the alb both on the skirt and on the wrists.

The stole is embroidered, and also the maniple, both of them having squared ends.

The pattern of the ornament on the amice and alb apparels, on the stole and on the maniple, is the same throughout, i.e. roses in circle.

The chasuble is of plain material, with a border ornament, but without an orphrey.

Peter de Lacy.  1375.  Northfleet.

## RALPH PERCHEHAY.

### 1378.

##### STIFFORD, ESSEX.

THE half-length effigy of a priest in mass vestments.

The amice is apparelled, having the fylfot ornament on it; while the sleeves of the alb are apparelled, having a quatrefoil as ornament.

The chasuble is of plain material, and is without orphrey or border ornament.

Part only of the maniple is to be seen.

The inscription is in black letter :—

"Orate ⁹p anima dn̅i̅ Radulphi perchehay quondam rectoris istius eccl̅i̅e̅ : "

Figure 26

RALPH PERCHEHAY. 1378. STIFFORD.

## (?) THOMAS CHERVYLL.

### c. 1380.

#### BEACHAMWELL, NORFOLK.

THE effigy of a priest in mass vestments.

The amice is apparelled, as is the alb both on the sleeves and on the skirt.

The maniple is embroidered its whole length, and, like the stole, has squared ends.

The chasuble is plain, and is without orphrey or border ornament.

Figure 27

Thomas Chervyll (?).   c. 1380.   Beachamwell.

## AN UNKNOWN PRIEST.

### *c.* 1390.

#### FULBOURN, CAMBRIDGESHIRE.

THE mutilated effigy of a priest in mass vestments. A tight-fitting cassock is visible at the wrists.

The amice is apparelled, as are the sleeves of the alb.

The maniple is, in this example, unornamented save for a line along its border and a quatrefoil at its lower end.

The chasuble is of plain material, without orphrey, but has a slight decoration on its border in the form of lines.

From the hands, which are joined in prayer, proceeds upwards a scroll, inscribed in black letter :—

"Sit laus deo : "

ANON. *c.* 1390. FULBOURN.

## JOHN DE SWYNSTEDE.

### 1395.

#### ASHRIDGE HOUSE, BUCKINGHAMSHIRE.

The effigy of a priest in mass vestments, now in private possession.

The amice is apparelled, as is the alb both on the sleeves and on the skirt. The shape of the latter apparel is unusual.

The maniple is narrow, with expanding ends, and is embroidered its whole length.

The stole is somewhat short, and also has expanding ends.

The chasuble is of plain material, without an orphrey, but with a border ornament.

A cassock with sleeves reaching over part of the hands, like mittens, is worn under the alb.

Encircling the head is a black letter inscription :—

" xp̄c dilexit nos & lauit nos a peccatis nr̄is in sanguine suo."

Figure 29

JOHN DE SWYNSTEDE. 1395. ASHRIDGE HOUSE.

## THOMAS GOMFREY.

### 1399.

#### DRONFIELD, DERBYSHIRE.

The effigy of a priest in mass vestments.

The sleeves of a tight-fitting cassock are visible at the wrists.

The amice is apparelled, as are the skirt and sleeves of the alb. The apparels on the sleeves are somewhat longer than is usual, and there seems to be a mistake in the engraving of the right sleeve of the alb.

The maniple has expanding ends, and is decorated its whole length with a running pattern.

The chasuble is of plain material, without an orphrey, but with a border ornament of quatrefoils.

The peculiarity of this brass, which it shares with that of his brother Richard Gomfrey in the same church, is the omission of the stole.

Thomas Gomfrey. 1399. Dronfield.

# ROBERT FYN.

## *c.* 1420.

### LITTLE EASTON, ESSEX.

The effigy of a priest in mass vestments.

The amice is apparelled, as is the alb, both on the sleeves and on the skirt.

The maniple is ornamented its whole length, and, like the stole, has slightly expanding ends.

The chasuble is of plain material, and has neither orphrey nor border ornament.

The inscription is in black letter :—

"In Northburgh Natus : Robertus ffyn vocitat'
De terra factus : in terram sum que redactus
Intercedendo : spiritum tibi x$\bar{p}$e comendo."

Figure 31

ROBERT FYN.   c. 1420.   LITTLE EASTON.

# WILLIAM BYSCHOPTON.

## 1432.

### GREAT BROMLEY, ESSEX.

The effigy of a priest in mass vestments.

The amice is apparelled, as is the alb both on the wrists and on the skirt; the sleeves of the cassock being visible below the alb.

The maniple is ornamented its whole length, as is the stole over the part which is visible below the chasuble.

The chasuble is of plain material, and without orphrey or border ornament.

From the head proceeds a scroll, inscribed in black letter :—

"Mater dei memento mei."

Below the feet is an inscription, part of which is lost, in black letter :—

"Quisquis eris qui transieris sta perlege plora : Sum quod eris [fueramque quod es pro me precor ora].

"Es testis xp̄e quod non iacet hic lapis iste : Corpus ut ornetur [sed spiritus ut memoretur]."

Figure 32

WILLIAM BYSCHOPTON. 1432. GREAT BROMLEY.

## JOHN BAKER.

### 1445.

#### FITZALAN CHAPEL, ARUNDEL.

The effigy of a priest in mass vestments.

The amice is apparelled, as are the sleeves and the skirt of the alb.

Part only of the maniple is to be seen, the rest being hidden by the chasuble.

The chasuble is of plain material, with an ornamented border, and a pillar orphrey which is decorated with the letters " I " and " ᙏ " in lozenge-shaped compartments, with roundels. The use of a personal ornament on the chasuble is unusual on brasses.

From the mouth proceeds a scroll, inscribed in black letter :—

" Miserere mei deus & salua me quia speraui in te."

JOHN BAKER. 1445. ARUNDEL.

## ESPERAUNCE BLONDELL.

### *c.* 1450.

#### FITZALAN CHAPEL, ARUNDEL.

THE half effigy of a priest in mass vestments.

The amice is apparelled, as are the sleeves of the alb. The maniple is ornamented with four-leaved flowers and roundels, as is also the apparel of the amice; while the ornamentation on the wrist apparels of the alb consists of a roundel.

The chasuble is of plain material, without orphrey or border ornament.

The inscription is in black letter :—

"Hic iacet dn̄s Esperaunce Blondell q̨nda
   Rector ecclie Suttōn : cui' aīe ꝑpiciet' de' amen."

Figure 34

Esperaunce Blondell.   c. 1450.   Arundel.

# JOHN SWETECOK.

## 1469.

#### LINGFIELD, SURREY.

The effigy of a priest in mass vestments.

The amice is apparelled; the chasuble is plain and without any ornamentation even at its border; the alb is apparelled at the wrists and on the skirt. The maniple and stole are embroidered with a leaf design. The close-fitting sleeves of the cassock are visible at the wrists below the alb.

The inscription is in black letter :—

"Orate ꝑ aĩa Johĩs Swetecok nuꝑ Mn̄i istius Collegij qui obiit xix
die Maij A° dn̄i millm̄o cccc° lxix°. Cui' aīe ꝓpicietur deus   Amen"

Figure 35

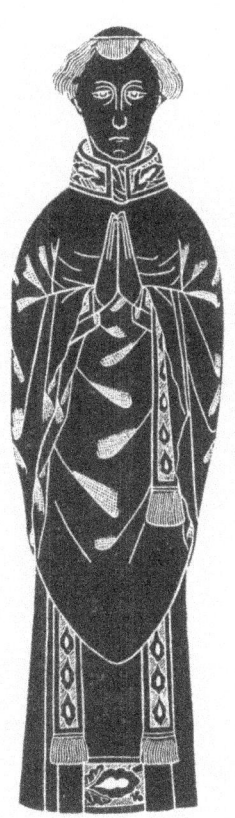

JOHN SWETECOK. 1469. LINGFIELD.

# AN UNKNOWN PRIEST

(*possibly John Kekilpeny, Rector from* 1461 *to* 1466). *c.* 1470.

LAINDON, ESSEX.

The effigy of a priest in mass vestments.

The amice is apparelled, as is the alb both on the sleeves and on the skirt.

The maniple is ornamented its whole length, as is the part of the stole visible below the chasuble.

The chasuble is of plain material, without orphrey or border ornament.

The sleeves of the cassock are visible below the alb.

In his hands is a mullet-footed chalice, with a Host inscribed i h c.

Figure 36

ANON. c. 1470. LAINDON.

## GEOFFREY BYSCHOP.

### 1477.

#### FULBOURN, CAMBRIDGESHIRE.

The effigy of a priest in mass vestments.

The amice is apparelled, as are the sleeves and skirt of the alb.

The maniple is embroidered its whole length.

The chasuble is of plain material, without an orphrey, but with an engrailed border ornament.

The hands are crossed downwards, as in the Flemish brass of Simon de Wenslagh, *c.* 1360, at Wensley (Fig. 81).

The foot inscription is in black letter :—

"Hic iacet Magister Gulfridus Byschop
quondam huius Ecclesiæ Vicarius qui obiit
secundo die Men. Nov$^r$. A°. dñi mcccc lxxvii.
Cuius animæ propicietur Dominus. Amen."

Figure 37

Geoffrey Byschop. 1477. Fulbourn.

# WALTER GAYNESFORD.

## 1493.

CARSHALTON, SURREY.

THE three-quarter length effigy of a priest in mass vestments, holding a chalice and Host marked with a cross in his hands.

The amice has a narrow apparel ; and the wide sleeves of the alb (under which the cassock is visible) are also apparelled.

The maniple is embroidered its whole length and is fringed.

Part of the stole appears below the chasuble.

The chasuble is of plain material, with a border ornament and with a narrow pillar orphrey.

Figure 38

WALTER GAYNESFORD. 1493. CARSHALTON.

# JOHN KNOYLL.

## 1503.

LINGFIELD, SURREY.

An effigy of a priest in mass vestments.
The amice is apparelled, as are the wide sleeves of the alb, and also the skirt of the alb.
The chasuble has an ornamented border.
The stole is narrow and embroidered, as is the maniple, which is not fringed. Both sides of the maniple are shown. The stole is shown with one end longer than the other.

By the side of the head is a black letter inscription :—

"Sctā trinitas un' de' miserere nobi$^s$."

Beneath the figure is a black letter inscription :—

"Here lyth Master Johñ knoyll sumtyme Master of
this coleg which Master Johñ decessid the iiij day of
July the yere of oure lord thoussand ccccc iij
on whose soull Ihū have mercy amen."

Figure 39

John Knoyll.   1503.   Lingfield.

# JOHN FRYE.

## 1507.

### NEW COLLEGE, OXFORD.

THE half-effigy of a priest in mass vestments, holding in his hands a chalice and Host.

The sleeves of the alb are wide and apparelled. Under the alb can be seen the sleeves of the cassock.

The amice is apparelled. Both sides of the embroidered maniple are visible.

The chasuble is of plain material, without an orphrey, but with a border ornament.

The inscription is in black letter :—

"Hic iacet Magist' Johēs ffrye quōdm̄ soci'
  hui' collegii et sacre theologie sholaris q' obiit
  viii° die mēs aplis a° dn̄i m° v° vii° cui' aīe ppiciet' de' a⁻ "

JOHN FRYE. 1507. NEW COLLEGE, OXFORD.

## AN UNKNOWN PRIEST.

### *c.* 1510.

#### LITTLEBURY, ESSEX.

THE effigy of a priest in mass vestments.

The amice is apparelled. Part of the apparel on the right sleeve of the alb is visible. The skirt of the alb also is apparelled, and bordered with lines.

The maniple is ornamented its whole length; and the embroidered stole is short.

The chasuble is of plain material, without an orphrey, but has two lines of ornament on the border.

In the hands of the effigy is a mullet-footed chalice, and Host inscribed ihs.

Figure 41

ANON.  *c.* 1510.  LITTLEBURY.

# JOHN GYLBERT.

## 1514.

### WINCHESTER COLLEGE, HAMPSHIRE.

THE three-quarter length effigy of a priest in mass vestments.

The amice is apparelled, and is partly covered by the chasuble.

The chasuble is of plain material, without an orphrey, but with a border ornament.

The maniple is straight and fringed, and embroidered its whole length, and covers the apparel on the wrist of the left sleeve of the alb. The apparel on the right sleeve is considerably larger than the usual representation on brasses.

Part of the embroidered stole appears, and is shown on the extreme right and left of the lower part of the chasuble.

The inscription is in black letter:—

"Orate p aīa dñi Johīs Gylbert olim socij istius collegij qui obijt xvi die mens' Julii A° dñi m° ccccc xiiij cuius aīe propicietur deus amē."

Figure 42

JOHN GYLBERT. 1514. WINCHESTER COLLEGE.

# WILLIAM WARDYSWORTH.

## 1533.

#### BETCHWORTH, SURREY.

The effigy of a priest in mass vestments, holding in his hands a mullet-footed chalice, with Host inscribed with the sacred monogram below a cross.

The amice is apparelled, as are also the sleeves and skirt of the alb, and both sleeves and skirt have lines at the border.

The maniple is embroidered its whole length.

The stole is long and narrow, hanging nearly to the ground on either side of the alb apparel.

The chasuble is of plain material, with lines for border ornament, and has a broad decorated pillar orphrey.

The inscription is in black letter :—

"Hic iacet dñs Willmus Wardysworth quondam
vicarius hui' ecclie qui obijt v$^{to}$ die Ianuarii Anno dni
m° cccccxxxiij° Cuius anime ppicietur deus amen"

Figure 43

WILLIAM WARDYSWORTH. 1533. BETCHWORTH.

# THOMAS CLERKE.

## c. 1411.

### HORSHAM, SUSSEX.

The mutilated effigy of a priest in processional vestments, the head and the lower part of the figure being lost.

The amice is apparelled, as is the alb, both on the skirt and on the sleeves.

The orphrey of the cope is ornamented with roses and quatrefoils in lozenges, and the priest's initials, T. and C., in circles.

The stole is crossed and embroidered its whole length.

The chief interest of the brass lies in the girding and looping of the alb at the waist; and in the wearing of the maniple, which is embroidered its whole length. Cf. the brass of John West, 1415, at Sudborough, Northamptonshire (Fig. 45).

Figure 44

THOMAS CLERKE. c. 1411. HORSHAM.

# JOHN WEST.

## 1415.

### SUDBOROUGH, NORTHAMPTONSHIRE.

THE effigy of a priest vested in apparelled amice; alb, which is apparelled on the skirt and on the sleeves; maniple, which is embroidered its whole length; and long crossed stole, which also is embroidered its whole length.

The alb is girded and looped up, as in the brass of Thomas Clerke, *c.* 1411, at Horsham, Sussex (Fig. 44); where the vestments are the same, with the addition of the cope.

JOHN WEST. 1415. SUDBOROUGH.

# WILLIAM DE ROTHEWELLE.

## c. 1361.

### ROTHWELL, NORTHAMPTONSHIRE.

The effigy of an archdeacon in processional vestments. The cassock, with a row of buttons, is visible at the wrists, while the bottom of the gown has a decorated border. He wears a surplice and an almuce, which has two pendants hanging down in front, but has not assumed the usual form of a cape, being represented instead as a small hood round the neck. The cope is a soft and full cloak fastened by a small brooch at the breast, and creased by being tight over the almuce. It has a narrow embroidered orphrey. There are indications that it had a large rolling hood, like the Cambridge Doctor of Divinity's cope of the present day.

Mr. Druitt (*Costume on Brasses*, p. 91 ; De La More Press, 1906) regards this cope as "a slightly ornamental form" of the *cappa nigra*, of which, however, there do not appear to be any other examples.

The cushion held by angels may be a sign of Flemish influence. Cf. the brass of Simon de Wenslagh, c. 1360, at Wensley (Fig. 81).

The inscriptions, which are in black letter, are :—

"Nūc xpē te peto mis'ere queso
qui venisti redim'e pditū
noli dāpnare me tuū redēpt'.
✠ Pur lalme William de Rothewelle qi ci est sepule jadis Erchidiakn de Essex Provendier de Croprych Ferryng et Yalmeton auonie Priez au Roy de glorie qe de lui eueyt pyte en honour de qi devoutement dites Pater noster et Aue."

Figure 46

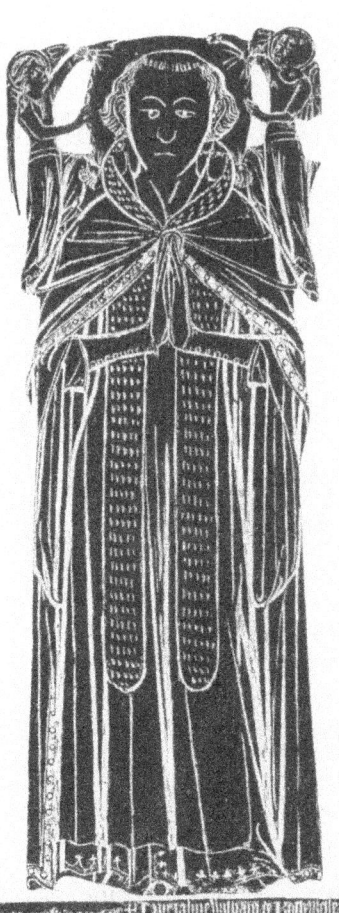

WILLIAM DE ROTHEWELLE. c. 1361. ROTHWELL.

# JOHN DE CAMPEDEN,

*Canon of Southwell and Warden of St. Cross.* 1382.

ST. CROSS, WINCHESTER, HAMPSHIRE.

The effigy of a canon in processional vestments.

He wears a cassock with tight sleeves, which are fastened with buttons; gown or pelisse; surplice reaching to the feet, the sleeves of which are almost entirely hidden by the cope; almuce, which is not represented as fur, and may be the black almuce; and cope.

The morse of the plain cope is ornamented with squares; while the orphrey bears roses and leopards' heads in lozenge-shaped compartments, together with halves of quatrefoils.

The hands are joined in prayer, and from them proceeds scrolls, in black letter :—

1. "Ihū cū venis iudicar' noli me cōdp̄nar'.
2. Qui plasmasti me miserere mei."

The foot inscription is in black letter :—

"Hic iacet Iohannes de Campedn̄ qndā custos istius hospitalis cuius āīe ppiciet' deus."

Above the head, on either side, are two shields, the one with the emblem of the Blessed Trinity, the other with the symbols of the Passion.

JOHN DE CAMPEDEN. 1382. ST. CROSS, WINCHESTER.

## MATTHEW DE ASSCHETON,

*Rector of Shillington and Walpole; Canon of York and Lincoln.* 1400.

### SHILLINGTON, BEDFORDSHIRE.

An effigy of a canon in processional vestments.

The cassock has tight sleeves fastened by a row of buttons at the wrists.

The surplice reaches to the feet, and has short sleeves.

The almuce has a hood and two pendants without tassels, but does not appear to have had a cape.

The cope is of plain material, with a morse and narrow orphrey ornamented with quatrefoils in lozenge-shaped compartments, together with roundels.

At the feet of the figure is a dog, an unusual representation on brasses of ecclesiastics.

Figure 48

Matthew de Asscheton. 1400. Shillington.

## WILLIAM ERMYN.

### 1401.

#### CASTLE ASHBY, NORTHAMPTONSHIRE.

The effigy of a priest in processional vestments, wearing cassock with tight sleeves buttoned at the wrists and reaching, like mittens, over part of the hands; surplice reaching to the feet; almuce, and cope. The morse of the cope contains (as do the shields on either side of the head) the Ermyn arms, "Ermine, a saltire gules, on the chief of the last a lion passant gardant or."

The orphrey of the cope contains figures of saints in embattled niches, each named in black letter:—

1 St. Anne.
2 St. Katharine.
3 St. Margaret.
4 St. Mary Magdalene.
5 St. Helena.

1 St. Peter.
2 St. Paul.
3 St. Andrew.
4 St. Nicholas.
5 St. Laurence.

Figure 49

WILLIAM ERMYN. 1401. CASTLE ASHBY.

# THOMAS AILEWARD.

## 1413.

#### HAVANT, HAMPSHIRE.

THE effigy of a priest in processional vestments. The sleeves of the gown or pelisse appear at the wrists. He wears a surplice with long sleeves, and almuce with hood and long pendants without tassels. The morse of the cope bears his initials " T. A."; while its orphrey is richly ornamented with heraldic charges, in circles and lozenges, viz. a garb, a rose, a fleur-de-lys, and a leopard's head, the series being repeated four and a half times on each orphrey.

The inscription is in black letter : —

" Hic iacet dn̄s Thomas Aileward quondm̄ Rector
istius Ecclīe qui obijt vi° die mensis Aprilis Anno
dn̄i Millō. cccc°. xiij° cui' āie ꝑpicietur deus Amen.
Sis testis xp̄e. quod non iacet hic lapis iste.
Corpus ut ornet' : sed mors vt p̄medicet'."

Below the inscription is a coat of arms [sa], a chevron between three garbs [or] for Aileward.

Figure 50

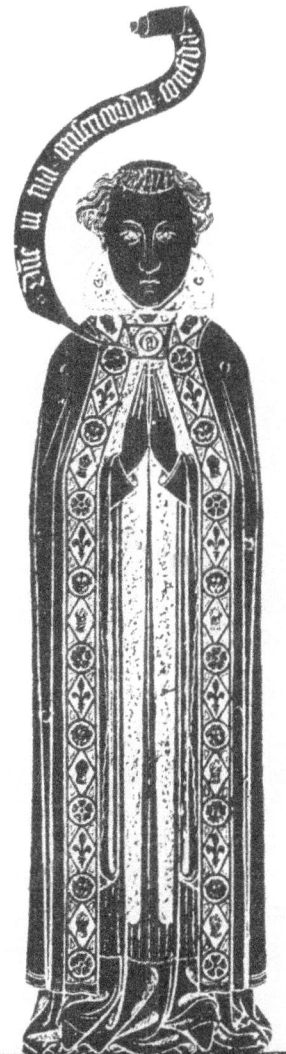

THOMAS AILEWARD. 1413. HAVANT.

# WILLIAM LANGETON.

## 1413.

#### EXETER CATHEDRAL, DEVONSHIRE.

THE side-view effigy of a kneeling canon in processional vestments, and wearing cassock, covering half the hands like mittens, gown, surplice, almuce, and shaped cope. The morse of the cope is ornamented with an x in a circle; while the orphreys are embroidered with the Stafford knot and the letter x in circles.

From the hands proceed a black-letter inscription:—

"Dne Ihu scdm actu meu noli me judicari . . ."

The inscription under the effigy is:—

"Hic iacet magister Willms langeton Consanguineus magit Edi Stafford Exon Epi quondm Canonicus huius Ecclie Qui obijt xxix° die mensis Januarij Anno dni Millmo CCCC° Terciodecimo. Cuius anime propicietur ompc deus Amen."

The shield is lowered so as to enable the brass to be shown on a larger scale.

Figure 51

WILLIAM LANGETON. 1413. EXETER CATHEDRAL.

# SIMON BACHE,

*Canon of St. Paul's.* 1414.

KNEBWORTH, HERTFORDSHIRE.

The effigy of a canon in processional vestments.

The tight sleeves of the cassock or gown can be seen at the wrists.

The surplice reaches to the feet, and has moderately long sleeves.

The almuce appears round the neck, with two pendants, without tassels, hanging down in front, and it has a cape, part of which can be seen above the left hand.

The cope is of richly-diapered material. Its morse bears a vernacle, while its orphrey is ornamented with figures of saints under canopies :—

| | |
|---|---|
| The Blessed Virgin Mary with our Lord. | St. John the Baptist with Lamb and flag. |
| St. Peter with a key. | St. Paul with a sword. |
| A Bishop with a pastoral staff. | An Archbishop with a cross. |
| St. Andrew with a cross saltire. | St. James with a staff. |

On either side of the head is a shield (lowered in the illustration) bearing a fess charged with three martlets.

Part of the black letter inscription, containing a prayer for the departed, has been cut away, probably to save the brass itself.

The part remaining reads :—

" Hic iacet dñs Simon Bache clicus quonda Thesaurari hospicii Illustrissimi
Principis dni henrici quinti Regis Angl'a chanonic' ecclie cathedralis sci pauli
londin q' obiit xix$^{mo}$ die maij A° dñi M° cccc° xiiii°."

Figure 52

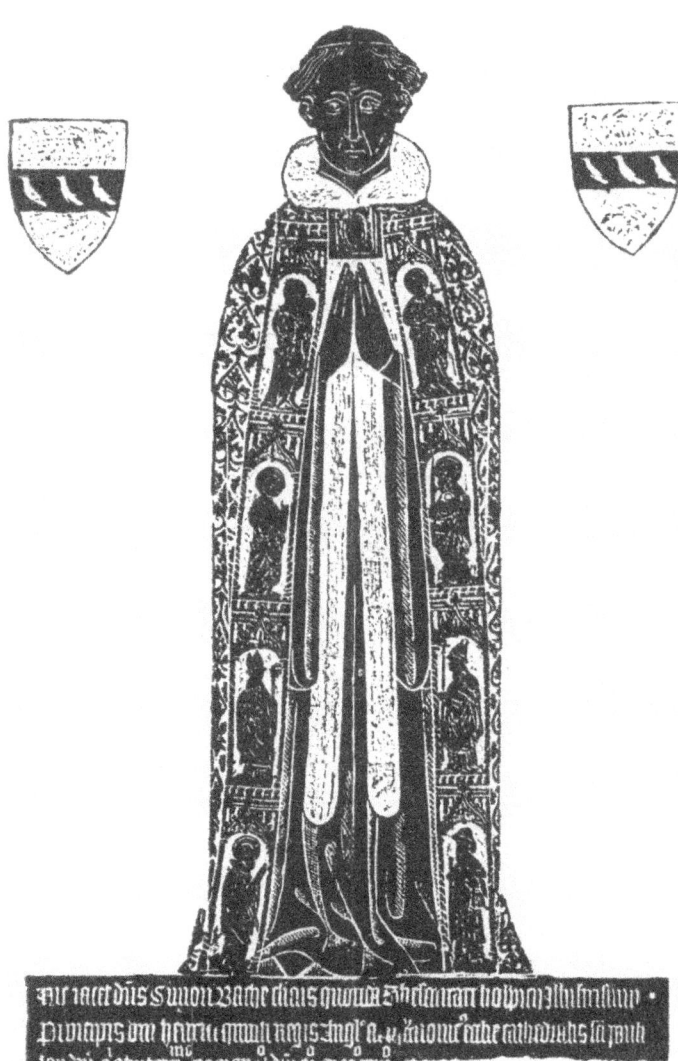

SIMON BACHE. 1414. KNEBWORTH.

119

# JOHN MAPILTON.

## 1432.

#### BROADWATER, SUSSEX.

THE effigy of a priest in processional vestments.

He wears a cassock which is visible at the wrists; gown or pelisse, the sleeves of which are lined with fur; surplice reaching to the feet, and with long sleeves; fur almuce, with hood; and shaped cope of plain material.

The morse of the cope bears the sacred monogram, and its orphrey is ornamented with circles and lozenges, which contain maple-leaves, the letter M, and roses.

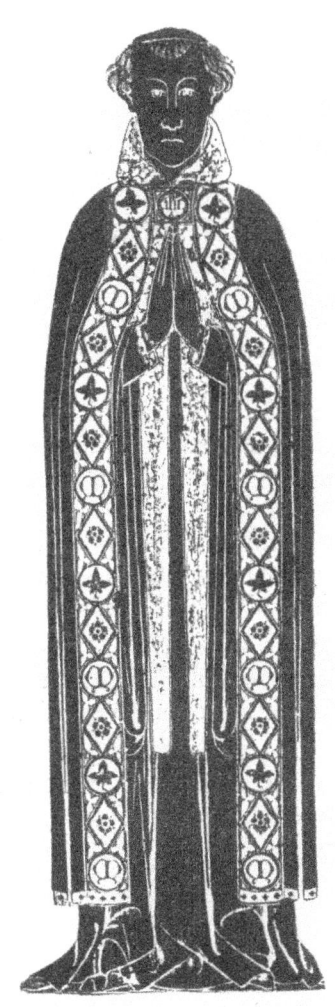

JOHN MAPILTON. 1432. BROADWATER.

# WILLIAM PRESTWYK.

## 1436.

### WARBLETON, SUSSEX.

THE effigy of a priest in processional vestments.

The cassock and the gown can be seen at the wrists.

The surplice is long, reaching to the feet, and has long sleeves.

The almuce has a hood and the usual pendants.

The cope is of plain material. Its morse bears the word "Credo," while along its orphrey runs an adaptation of the words of Job xix. 25, 26 :—

"Quod redemptor meus viuit Et in nouissimo die de terra surrecturus sum Et in carne mea videbo deū sauatorem (*sic*) meum"

The bottom of the cope is ornamented with a border marked with roundels.

Figure 54

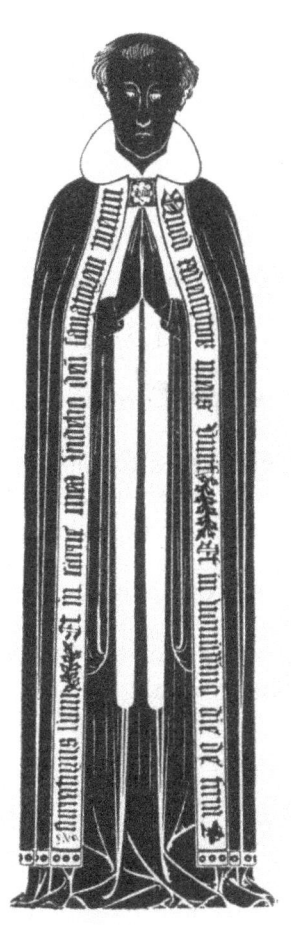

WILLIAM PRESTWYK. 1436. WARBLETON.

# THOMAS TONGE.

## 1472.

#### BEEFORD, YORKSHIRE.

The effigy of a priest vested for procession.

He wears an alb which is apparelled on the skirt; apparelled amice; and cope of richly-figured material with a narrow orphrey.

The morse of the cope is hidden by the book which he holds in his hands.

The alb is looped up, but the crossed stole is not worn, nor can the maniple be seen.

Figure 55

Thomas Tonge. 1472. Beeford.

# (?) JOHN GYGER.

### *c.* 1510.

#### TATTERSHALL, LINCOLNSHIRE.

The effigy of a priest in processional vestments.

He wears a pointed *pileus* on his head; a cassock with close sleeves; gown or pelisse, which has fur cuffs; surplice with short sleeves; almuce with cape and pendants with tassels; and cope of plain material.

The large square morse of the cope contains a half-effigy of our Lord in glory, and the orphrey is ornamented with twelve figures of Apostles, each under a canopy, and all, except St. John, holding books in their hands, those of St. Andrew, St. Bartholomew, and St. Thomas being in cases, the necks of which are grasped by the fingers. The lower part of the cope is turned back, hiding part of the lowest pair of figures on the orphrey.

The figures are arranged in the following order:—

| | |
|---|---|
| St. Peter with the keys. | St. Paul with a sword. |
| St. Andrew with a cross saltire. | St. John with a chalice and serpent. |
| St. James the Great with a staff, and a badge on his hat. | St. Jude with a cross staff. |
| St. James the Less with a club. | St. Simon with a saw. |
| St. Bartholomew with a flaying-knife. | St. Matthew with an axe. |
| St. Philip with three loaves in his hand. | St. Thomas with a spear. |

Figure 56

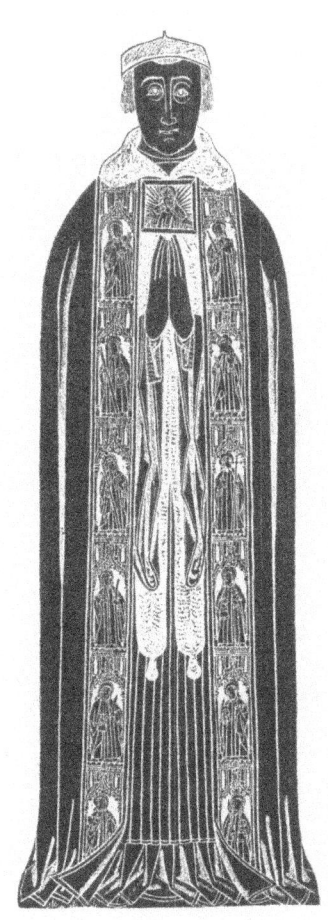

JOHN GYGER (?) c. 1510. TATTERSHALL.

## GABRIEL SILVESTER.

### 1512.

**CROYDON, SURREY.**

THE effigy of a priest in processional vestments. He wears a cassock, which is visible at the wrists ; gown or pelisse with wide sleeves turned back and showing the fur lining ; surplice ; almuce with long pendants ending in tassels ; and cope which has an ornamented border. The morse is represented as jewelled.

The inscription is in black letter :—

"Siluester Gabriel cuius lapis hic tegit ossa
    vera sacerdotum gloria nuper erat.
legis nemo sacre diuina volumina verbis
    Clarius aut vita sanctius explicuit.
Cominus ergo deū modo felix eminus almis
    Qeuē pius in scriptis viderat ante videt.
Anno dñi millm̄o v° xij° iiij° die octobr' vita est funct'."

Figure 57

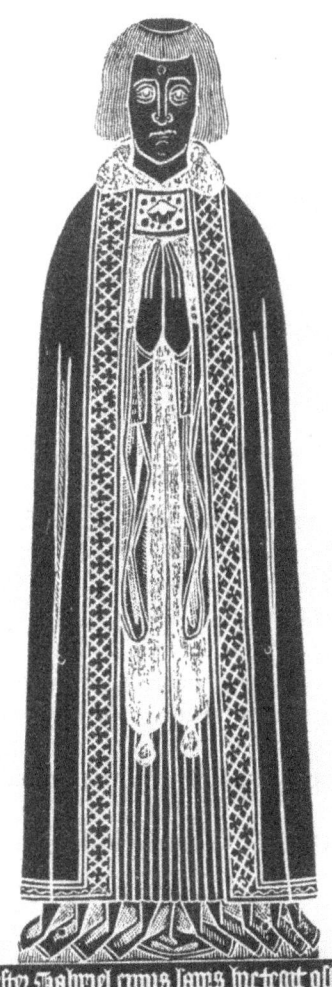

GABRIEL SILVESTER. 1512. CROYDON.

## ROBERT LANGTON, D.D.

### 1518.

#### QUEEN'S COLLEGE, OXFORD.

THE effigy of a priest wearing cassock, buttoned at the wrists; gown, the sleeves of which are lined with fur; long surplice, almuce, and cope.

The almuce has a hood, and tassels to its pendants.

The cope is ornamented with a diaper of lozenges containing fleurs-de-lys; the narrow orphrey being decorated with half-lozenges containing double-rayed semicircles within waved lines.

The morse bears a blazing sun surcharged with a Tudor rose.

On the head is a round-pointed doctor's cap—the pointed *pileus*.

Robert Langton. 1518. Queen's College, Oxford.

# JOHN WHITE.

## *c.* 1548.

### WINCHESTER COLLEGE, HAMPSHIRE.

A PORTION of a palimpsest brass, the reverse of which shows part of the figure of a lady in widow's dress, *c.* 1440.

The bishop wears a tight-fitting cassock, a gown with wide sleeves lined with fur, almuce with cape and pendants, surplice with long sleeves, and cope.

On the morse of the cope is IHS in a circle. The material of the cope is ornamented with scroll-work and pomegranates, and its orphrey with alternate roses and marguerites, each being in a diamond-shaped border.

The hood of the cope can just be noticed on either side of the top portion of the orphrey, and would appear to have been suspended below the orphrey, not over it.

The brass was laid down about 1548; but White was Bishop of Lincoln from 1554 to 1556, and of Winchester from 1556 to 1559. He is described in the *Dictionary of English Church History* as "a scholar and supporter of Queen Mary and a persecutor of Protestants; deprived by Elizabeth, whom he insulted at Mary's funeral sermon." He died in 1560.

Figure 59

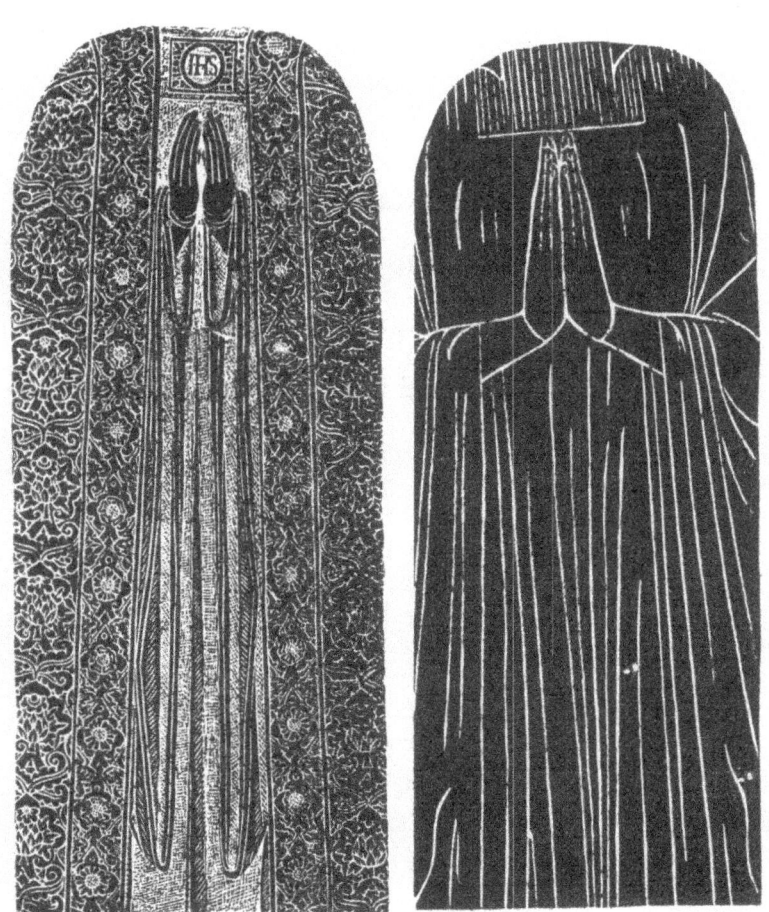

JOHN WHITE.  c. 1548.  WINCHESTER COLLEGE.

# THOMAS COD.

## 1465.

ST. MARGARET'S CHURCH, ROCHESTER, KENT.

The palimpsest brass of a priest, who is shown in two sets of vestments.

On the one side he is represented in cassock, which is visible at the wrists, gown, surplice, almuce, and cope of plain material.

The morse of the cope has a quatrefoil in a lozenge, and its orphrey is ornamented with leaves in heart-shaped compartments, alternating with i h̄ u and m c̄y in black letter, in circles.

On the other side he is represented in gown with cuffs, surplice, cope, and apparelled amice in place of the almuce.

The morse bears a quatrefoil, and the orphrey is ornamented with a running design of leaves.

Figure 60

Thomas Cod. 1465. St. Margaret's, Rochester.

# EDWARD TACHAM.

## 1473.

### WINCHESTER COLLEGE, HAMPSHIRE.

The half-effigy of a priest wearing gown, surplice, cope, and amice.

The cope is of plain material, with a broad decorated morse, while the narrow orphrey is ornamented with cross crosslets.

The amice, which takes the place of the almuce, is apparelled.

The foot inscription is in black letter :—

"Orate pro aīa Magistri Edwardi Tachm̄ quondā socij
istius Collegij qui obijt xvii° die Marcij Anno dn̄i
Millm° CCCC° lxxiij°. Cuius aīe ṗpicietur deus Amen."

Figure 61

Edward Tacham. 1473. Winchester College.

# JOHN LOVELLE.

## 1438.

### ST. GEORGE'S CHURCH, CANTERBURY, KENT.

The effigy of a priest in processional vestments, with his head lying on a cushion with six tassels.

He wears gown, surplice, and shaped cope of plain material.

The morse and orphrey of the cope are ornamented with quatrefoils.

In this example the almuce is not, as is usually the case, worn with the cope.

The inscription is in black letter:—

"Hic requiescit dñs Johēs lovelle quondā Rector isti' Ecclīe qui obijt xxiiii die mensis Aprilis anno dnī millo CCCC° xxxviii° Cuius āīe ppiciet' deus Amē."

Figure 62

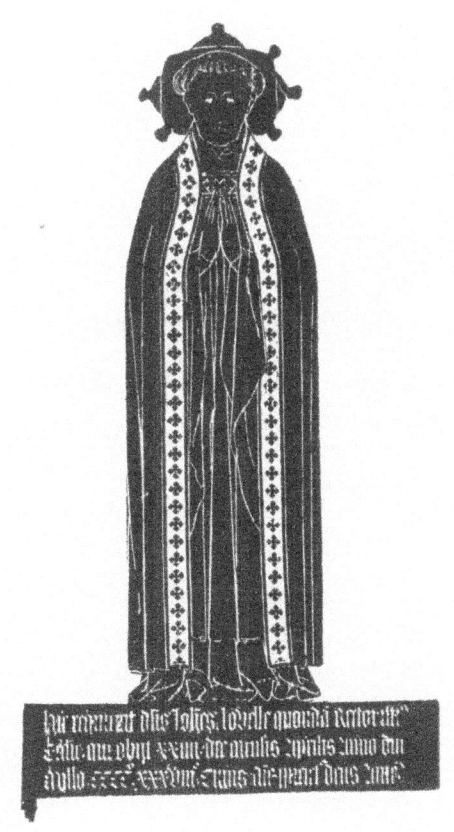

JOHN LOVELLE. 1438. ST. GEORGE'S, CANTERBURY.

## WILLIAM KIRKEBY.

### 1458.

#### THEYDON GERNON, ESSEX.

The effigy of a priest wearing cassock, gown, surplice with long sleeves, and shaped cope.

The surplice is shown as gathered at the neck; while the morse of the cope is ornamented with a quatrefoil, and its orphrey with a floriated pattern.

The almuce is not worn with the cope in this example.

Over the priest's head is a shield bearing—

"(azure) five lions rampant (or), on a canton (argent) a pierced mullet of six points (gules) for Kirkeby."

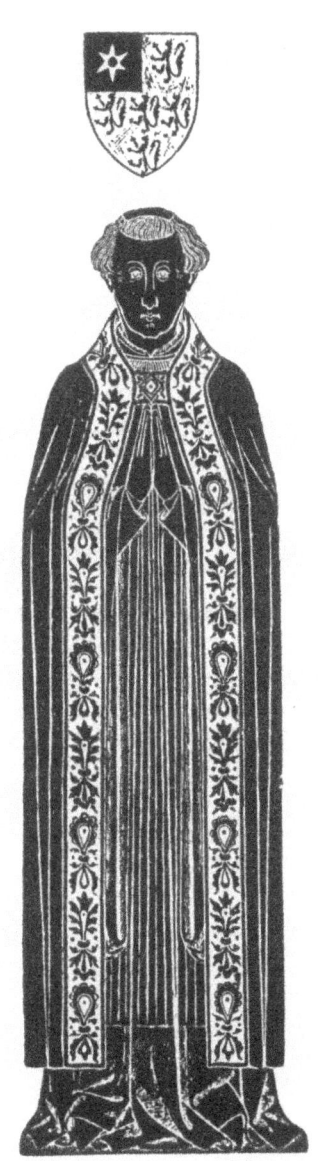

WILLIAM KIRKEBY. 1458. THEYDON GERNON.

## AN UNKNOWN PRIEST.

### c. 1460.

#### TEMPLE CHURCH, BRISTOL.

The effigy of a priest in cassock, surplice with long sleeves, and shaped cope, the orphrey of which is ornamented with a running pattern, and its morse with a cross. The almuce is, in this example, omitted, as in the brass of John Lovelle, 1438, in St. George's Church, Canterbury (see Fig. 62).

Figure 64

Anon. c. 1460. Temple Church, Bristol.

# WILLIAM TANNER.

## 1418.

**COBHAM, KENT.**

THE half-length effigy of a priest in cassock, gown, surplice, and almuce.

The almuce has a hood, and two tassels on the bottom of its cape. It is fastened at the breast with a lozenge-shaped brooch.

The inscription is in black letter:—

"Hic iacet Willm̄s Tannere qui prim' obiit Magister istius Collegii xxij° die Mensis Junij Anno dn̄i M° cccc° xviij° cuius Anime propicietur dns Amen."

Figure 65

WILLIAM TANNER. 1418. COBHAM.

# THOMAS TEYLAR.

## *c.* 1480.

#### BYFLEET, SURREY.

The effigy of a priest wearing a cassock, which is visible at the wrists; gown; surplice with long sleeves; and fur almuce.

The almuce has a cape with six tassels, and two pendants with tassels.

The inscription is in black letter :—

"Hic iacet Thoṁs Teylar Rector ecclīe pochialis de Biflete et vnus canonicor' ecclīe Cathedralis lincōln̄ qui quidm̄ Thoṁs obiit . . . die mensis. . . . A° dn̄i millīo CCCC° lxxx. . . . Cuius Anime ꝑpiciet' de' "

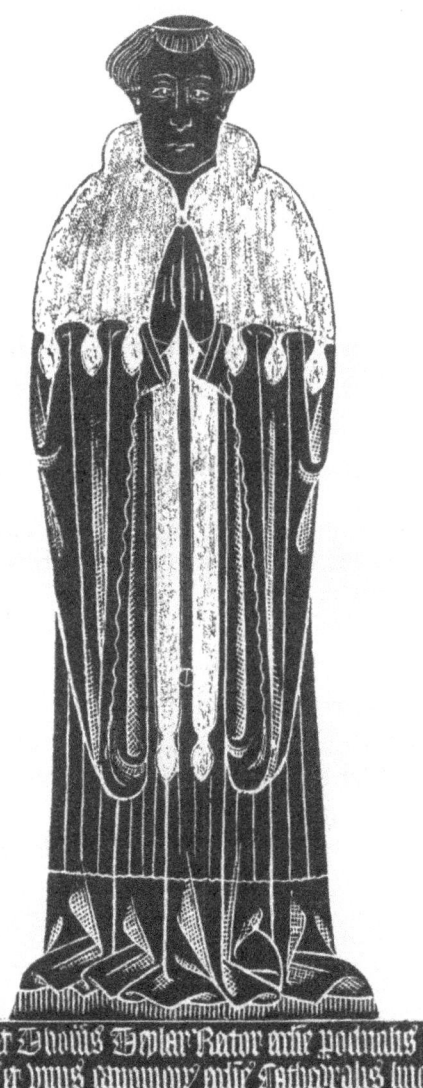

Figure 66

Thomas Teylar. c. 1480. Byfleet.

# RICHARD HARWARD.

## 1493.

### ST. CROSS, WINCHESTER, HAMPSHIRE.

THE effigy of a priest wearing a small round cap (*pileus*) with a point at the top ; gown with narrow fur cuffs ; surplice ; and almuce.

The almuce has a hood, cape with nine tassels, and pendants with tassels.

The foot inscription, which is a modern restoration, is in black letter :—

"Orate p aīa Mri Ricardi Harward decretorum doctoris ac nuper huius hospitalis magistri qui obiit . . . die Aprilis A° dn̄i M° cccc° nonogesimo tertio. Cuj' āre ppicietur deus"

Figure 67

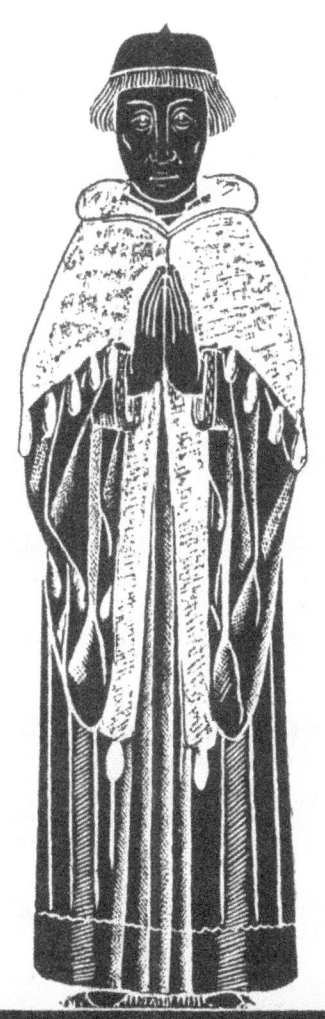

RICHARD HARWARD. 1493. ST. CROSS, WINCHESTER.

# RALPH ELCOK.

## 1510.

#### TONG, SHROPSHIRE.

The effigy of a priest in gown or pelisse with wide sleeves; long surplice; and almuce.

The almuce has the usual pendants, but has not the usual full cape-shape appearance.

The inscription is in black letter:—

" Hic iacet Radulph' Elcok celre cōfrat' isti' colegii
qui natus fuit in villa stopfordie infra comitatu
Cestrie qui obiit in festo scē katerine Virginis
et marter Anno dnī millm̄o CCCCC° desimo."

Figure 68

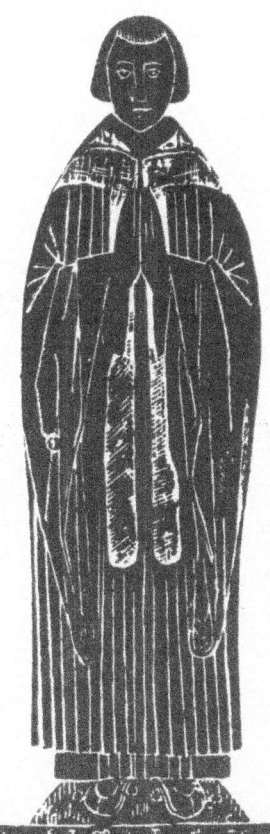

Ralph Elcok. 1510. Tong.

# RICHARD ADAMS.

## 1522.

### EAST MALLING, KENT.

The effigy of a priest in gown, surplice, and almuce.

The almuce has tassels on the bottom of its cape and on its pendants.

A mullet-footed chalice, and Host marked with a cross crosslet, are held in the hands.

Figure 69

RICHARD ADAMS. 1522. EAST MALLING.

# ROBERT HACOMBLEYN.

## 1528.

### KING'S COLLEGE, CAMBRIDGE.

THE effigy of a priest in gown or pelisse which has loose sleeves lined with fur, surplice with full sleeves, and almuce which is realistically represented as a fur cape, but without the usual pendants.

From the hands proceed a scroll, bearing in black letter:—

"Vuln'a x$\bar{\text{p}}$e tua : michi dulcis sint medicina."

Figure 70

ROBERT HACOMBLEYN. 1528.
KING'S COLLEGE, CAMBRIDGE.

# JAMES COORTHOPP,

*Dean of Peterborough.* 1557.

CHRIST CHURCH, OXFORD.

THE effigy of a priest wearing a cassock with tight sleeves visible at the wrists; gown or pelisse, open in front below the surplice; surplice, which is gathered at the neck and has short sleeves; and almuce.

The almuce has the usual pendants, and the cape portion appears to be gathered up over the arms, while it reaches at the sides to below the waist. It, like the pendants, is tasselled.

Figure 71

JAMES COORTHOPP. 1557. CHRIST CHURCH, OXFORD.

## AN UNKNOWN PRIEST.

### *c.* 1370.

**WATTON, HERTFORDSHIRE.**

THE effigy of a priest who is vested in cassock with close sleeves, surplice with short sleeves, almuce, and choral cope.

The almuce is not represented as of fur, but may be meant for the black fur almuce. It has a hood and pendants.

The feet rest on a lion.

Figure 72

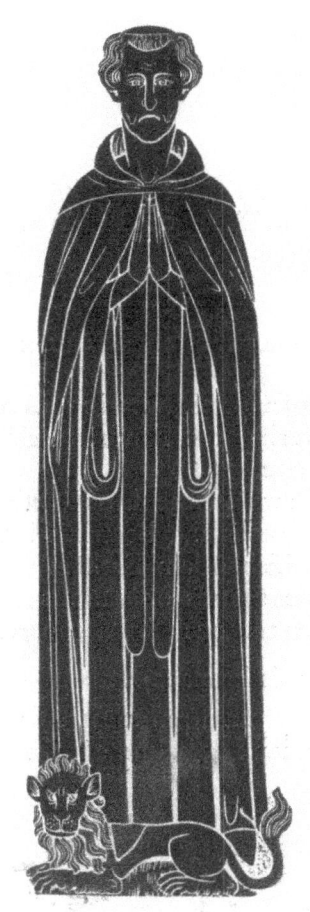

ANON. c. 1370. WATTON.

# ADAM ERTHAM.

## 1382.

#### FITZALAN CHAPEL, ARUNDEL.

THE half-effigy of a priest wearing a cassock with close sleeves partly covering the hands, black almuce, surplice, and black choral cope.

Attention is drawn in the Introduction to the fact that on the tomb of Thomas and Beatrix Fitzalan in the chapel of the college of which Adam Ertham was the first master, all but one of the figures of canons in the choral cope wear it fastened at the neck by a morse.

The inscription is in black letter :—

"Sir Adm̄ Ertham pm mestre de cest College gist ẏcẏ dieux de salme eẏt m̄cẏ amen."

Figure 73

Adam Ertham. 1382. Arundel.

# NICHOLAS OF LOUTH.

## 1383.

### COTTINGHAM, YORKSHIRE.

THE effigy of the rector, and builder of the chancel, of Cottingham Church.

He wears a cassock which partly covers the hands and is fastened at the wrists by a row of buttons; surplice; almuce (probably the black fur almuce) with hood and pendants; and over all the black choral cope.

Cottingham, transferred to Haltemprice, was a house of Augustinian Canons; and this brass, like the next illustration, may represent the choir habit of an Augustinian canon.

Figure 74

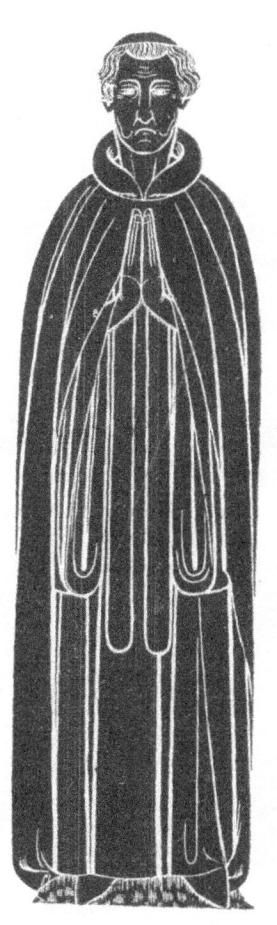

Nicholas of Louth.   1383.   Cottingham.

## RICHARD BEWFFORESTE.

### *c.* 1510.

#### DORCHESTER, OXFORDSHIRE.

THE effigy of an abbot of the Augustinian or Black Canons in his choir habit.

He wears a cassock; long surplice; fur almuce, with hood, cape, and tasselled pendants; and what is either a plain cope-like cloak with hood, or the black choral cope.

His pastoral staff is between his right arm and his body.

The incription is in black letter :—

"Here lyeth sir Richard Bewfforeste
pray ihū geve his sowle good Rest"

Figure 75

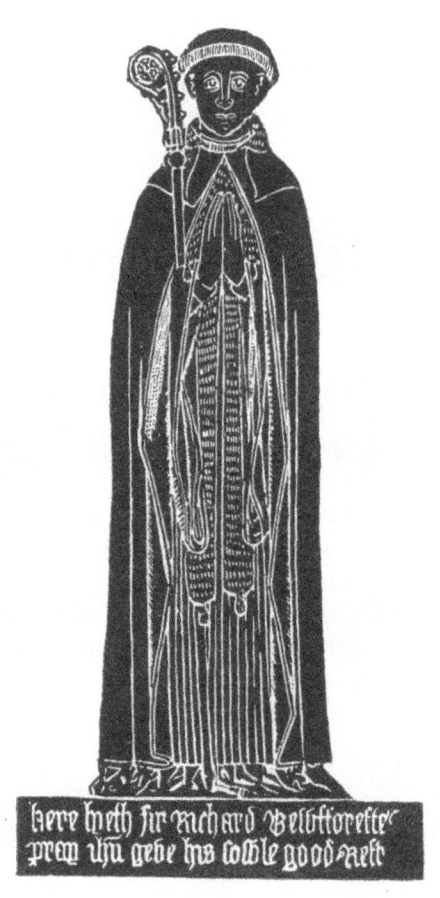

Richard Bewfforeste.   c. 1510.   Dorchester, Oxon.

## WILLIAM LAWNDER.

### *c.* 1530.

#### NORTHLEACH, GLOUCESTERSHIRE.

The side-view effigy of a priest kneeling sideways at a desk.

He wears a cassock, which can be seen at the wrists; and over this a gown, which has wide sleeves turned up, with fur lining; and over this the surplice, with full sleeves which are turned back at the wrists.

The hood is thrown over the shoulders, the liripipe being fastened to the left side with a brooch.

Figure 76

WILLIAM LAWNDER. c. 1530. NORTHLEACH.

## ST. STEPHEN AS A DEACON.

### 1337.

#### HIGHAM FERRARS, NORTHAMPTONSHIRE.

THE figure of St. Stephen as a deacon on the brass to Laurence St. Maur at Higham Ferrars (Fig. 21). St. Stephen is vested in apparelled amice, and an alb without apparels. The maniple is not embroidered; and the dalmatic, which is of plain material, is fringed on both sides and at the bottom. In his right hand are stones on a long cloth, to which he is pointing with his left hand.

Figure 77

St. Stephen. 1337. Higham Ferrars.

# ROGER PARKERS.

## *c.* 1370.

#### NORTH STOKE, OXFORDSHIRE.

The headless half-effigy of a priest in cassock, which is buttoned at the wrists; over which is the mantle of the Order of the Garter, fastened at the neck with a tasselled cord passing through two pairs of lace holes, and falling down in front. The mantle has a plain narrow border round the neck and edges. On the left shoulder is a round badge bearing the Cross of St. George, and formerly enamelled red on a white ground.

The inscription is in black letter :—

" Hic iacet rogerus parkers quōdā rector istī' ecclie : et canonicus capelle de Wȳndsores : cui' aīe ppicietur deus "

Figure 78

Roger Parkers. c. 1370. North Stoke.

## ROGER LUPTON, LL.D.

### 1540.

#### ETON COLLEGE, BUCKINGHAMSHIRE.

THE effigy of a priest wearing a cassock which is visible at the wrists; gown or pelisse, with wide sleeves which are represented as lined with fur ; and the mantle of the Order of the Garter, with a St. George's Cross on the left shoulder, the mantle being fastened at the neck by a button bearing a quatrefoil ornament.

From the hands proceed a scroll, bearing in black letter :—

"Miserere mei deus secundum magnam misericordiam tuam."

Figure 79

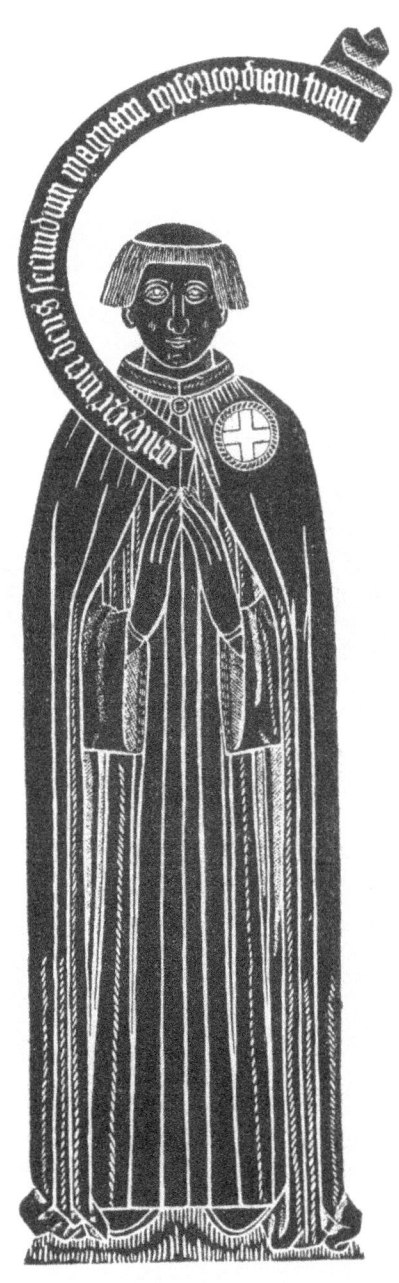

Roger Lupton. 1540. Eton College.

# ARTHUR COLE.

## 1558.

MAGDALEN COLLEGE, OXFORD.

THE effigy of a priest wearing a cassock, the sleeves of which are visible at the wrists; gown, which has wide sleeves, surplice with very short sleeves; almuce; and mantle of the Order of the Garter.

The almuce hangs round the neck in a form not unlike an apparelled amice; but is not of the usual cape form, extending instead to the knees.

The mantle of the Order of the Garter has a St. George's Cross on the left shoulder. It is fastened at the neck with a button or brooch, from which hang long cords, ending in tassels.

Figure 80

ARTHUR COLE. 1558. MAGDALEN COLLEGE, OXFORD.

# SIMON DE WENSLAGH.

## c. 1360.

### WENSLEY, YORKSHIRE.

An example of the Flemish brass of a priest in mass vestments.

The hands are crossed downwards upon the body, a chalice with a circular base, and a paten, lying upon the breast, over the arms. With this may be compared the Flemish brass of (?) Thomas de Horton, c. 1360, at North Mimms, Hertfordshire, where the chalice and paten are below the hands (Fig. 82).

The head rests upon a cushion supported by two angels in apparelled albs.

At the feet are two dogs.

The alb is richly apparelled both on the skirt and on the sleeves, the latter apparels encircling the wrists, as in English brasses of the first half of the fourteenth century.

The amice is apparelled and lies low on the neck.

The maniple is embroidered its whole length ; and the ends of the stole appear below the chasuble.

The chasuble is of plain material with an ornamented border and embroidered Y-shaped orphrey.

The ornamentation of the vestments consists of circular compartments containing grotesque animals alternating with lozenge-shaped compartments filled with quatrefoils.

Simon de Wenslagh.   c. 1360.   Wensley.

# (?) THOMAS DE HORTON.

### c. 1360.

#### NORTH MIMMS, HERTFORDSHIRE.

A FLEMISH brass representing a priest in mass vestments, with a chalice and paten lying on his breast below his hands ; cf. the Flemish brass of Simon de Wenslagh, c. 1360, at Wensley (Fig. 81).

The apparel of the amice is richly embroidered and hangs low on the neck.

The alb is apparelled on the skirt and on the sleeves, the latter apparel encircling the wrists.

The chasuble is of plain material and has a Y-shaped orphrey and an ornamented border.

The maniple is ornamented its whole length, and the ends of the embroidered stole appear below the chasuble.

The feet rest on a stag.

Thomas de Horton (?). c. 1360.
North Mimms.

# THOMAS DELAMARE.

## *c.* 1375.

### ST. ALBANS ABBEY, HERTFORDSHIRE.

A LARGE Flemish brass of an abbot of St. Albans in mass vestments. He wears a mitre which is decorated with leaves and with two medallions containing beads. The *infulae* are not visible. The amice is apparelled, the ornament consisting of griffins, and it lies low on the neck. The chasuble is of plain material with an ornamented border and a Ψ-shaped orphrey which is decorated with heads in circles and with leaves. The maniple is embroidered its whole length with quatrefoils and with lions' heads in circles. On the hands, which are crossed downwards, are jewelled gloves. The dalmatic is of plain material with an ornamented border, and under it is the tunicle, below which are the fringed ends of the stole. The apparel on the skirt of the alb is ornamented with animals. On the feet are sandals covered with embroidery. The head of the pastoral staff, which has no *vexillum*, contains an *Agnus Dei*. The feet rest on two animals fighting. Above and around the figure is canopy work containing figures. Over the head is the First Person of the Trinity seated, and on either side angels with censers and musical instruments. Beyond these are St. Peter on the left with a key, and St. Paul on the right with a sword. In the shafts of the canopy are fourteen figures, seven on each side.

|  | St. Alban with cross and sword. | St Oswyn with crown on head and a spear in his hand. | |
|---|---|---|---|
| Daniel | St John the Evangelist with chalice and serpent. | St. James the Great with a scallop shell. | Isaiah |
| David | St. Andrew with a cross saltire. | St Bartholomew with a flaying-knife. | Haggai |
| Hosea. | St. Thomas with a spear. | St. Philip with a loaf. | Joel |

Of the evangelistic symbols in the four corners of the fillet inscription that of St. John has been lost.

The marginal inscription is :—" ✠ Hic iacet dominus Thomas quondam abbas huius monesterii."

A space, never filled in, has been left for the date of his death, the brass having been made in his lifetime.

Figure 83

THOMAS DELAMARE.  c. 1375.  ST. ALBANS ABBEY.

# INDEX OF PERSONS

|  |  |  | FIG |
|---|---|---|---|
| Adams, Richard | East Malling | 1522 | 69 |
| Aileward, Thomas | Havant | 1413 | 50 |
| Anon. | Bristol (Temple Church) | c 1460 | 64 |
| Anon | Fulbourn | c. 1390 | 28 |
| Anon. | Laindon | c. 1470 | 36 |
| Anon. | Littlebury | c. 1510 | 41 |
| Anon. | Shottesbrooke | c. 1370 | 24 |
| Anon. | Stoke-in-Teignhead | c. 1320 | 19 |
| Anon. | Watton | c. 1370 | 72 |
| Asscheton, Matthew de | Shillington | 1400 | 48 |
| | | | |
| Bache, Simon | Knebworth | 1414 | 52 |
| Bacon, Adam de | Oulton (formerly at) | c. 1310 | 16 |
| Baker, John | Arundel | 1445 | 33 |
| Bell, Richard | Carlisle Cathedral | 1496 | 8 |
| Beltoun, Richard de | Corringham | c. 1340 | 23 |
| Bewfforeste, Richard | Dorchester (Oxon) | c 1510 | 75 |
| Blondell, Esperaunce | Arundel | c. 1450 | 34 |
| Bowthe, John | East Horsley | 1478 | 7 |
| Byschop, Geoffrey | Fulbourn | 1477 | 37 |
| Byschopton, William | Great Bromley | 1432 | 32 |
| | | | |
| Campeden, John de | Winchester (St. Cross) | 1382 | 47 |
| Chervyll, Thomas (?) | Beachamwell | c. 1380 | 27 |
| Clerke, Thomas | Horsham | c 1411 | 44 |
| Cod, Thomas | Rochester (St. Margaret's) | 1465 | 60 |
| Cole, Arthur | Oxford (Magdalen Coll.) | 1558 | 80 |
| Coorthopp, James | „ (Christ Church) | 1557 | 71 |
| Cranley, Thomas | „ (New College) | 1417 | 3 |
| | | | |
| Delamare, Thomas | St. Albans Abbey | c. 1375 | 83 |
| | | | |
| Elcok, Ralph | Tong | 1510 | 68 |
| Ermyn, William | Castle Ashby | 1401 | 49 |
| Ertham, Adam | Arundel | 1382 | 73 |
| Estney, John | Westminster Abbey | 1498 | 14 |
| | | | |
| Frye, John | Oxford (New College) | 1507 | 40 |
| Fyn, Robert | Little Easton | c 1420 | 31 |

## The Ornaments of the Ministers

|  |  |  | FIG |
|---|---|---|---|
| Gaynesford, Walter | Carshalton | 1493 | 38 |
| Geste, Edmund | Salisbury Cathedral | 1578 | 11 |
| Gomfrey, Thomas | Dronfield | 1399 | 30 |
| Goodryke, Thomas | Ely Cathedral | 1554 | 10 |
| Gore, Nichol de | Woodchurch | c. 1330 | 20 |
| Grenefeld, William de | York Minster | 1315 | 1 |
| Grofhurst, Henry de | Horsemonden | c. 1340 | 22 |
| Gyger, John (?) | Tattershall | c. 1510 | 56 |
| Gylbert, John | Winchester College | 1514 | 42 |
| Hacombleyn, Robert | Cambridge (King's Coll.) | 1528 | 70 |
| Hakebourne, Richard de | Oxford (Merton College) | c. 1311 | 17 |
| Harsnett, Samuel | Chigwell | 1631 | 4 |
| Harward, Richard | Winchester (St. Cross) | 1493 | 67 |
| Hop, Thomas de | Kemsing | c. 1320 | 18 |
| Horton, Thomas de (?) | North Mimms | c. 1360 | 82 |
| Kirkeby, William | Theydon Gernon | 1458 | 63 |
| Knoyll, John | Lingfield | 1503 | 39 |
| Lacy, Peter de | Northfleet | 1375 | 25 |
| Langeton, William | Exeter Cathedral | 1413 | 51 |
| Langton, Robert | Oxford (Queen's College) | 1518 | 58 |
| Lawnder, William | Northleach | c. 1530 | 76 |
| Louth, Nicholas of | Cottingham | 1383 | 74 |
| Lovelle, John | Canterbury (St George's) | 1438 | 62 |
| Lupton, Roger | Eton College | 1540 | 79 |
| Mapilton, John | Broadwater | 1432 | 53 |
| Parkers, Roger | North Stoke | c. 1370 | 78 |
| Perchehay, Ralph | Stifford | 1378 | 26 |
| Prestwyk, William | Warbleton | 1436 | 54 |
| Pursglove, Robert | Tideswell | 1579 | 12 |
| Robinson, Henry | Oxford (Queen's College) | 1616 | 13 |
| Rothewelle, William de | Rothwell | c. 1361 | 46 |
| St. Maur, Laurence | Higham Ferrars | 1337 | 21 |
| St. Stephen | Higham Ferrars | 1337 | 77 |
| Silvester, Gabriel | Croydon | 1512 | 57 |
| Swetecok, John | Lingfield | 1469 | 35 |
| Swynstede, John de | Ashridge House | 1395 | 29 |
| Tacham, Edward | Winchester College | 1473 | 61 |
| Tanner, William | Cobham | 1418 | 65 |
| Teylar, Thomas | Byfleet | c. 1480 | 66 |
| Tonge, Thomas | Beeford | 1472 | 55 |
| Trilleck, John | Hereford Cathedral | 1360 | 5 |

## AS SHOWN ON ENGLISH MONUMENTAL BRASSES

|  |  |  | FIG |
|---|---|---|---|
| Waldeby, Robert de | Westminster Abbey | 1397 | 2 |
| Waltham, John de | Westminster Abbey | 1395 | 6 |
| Wardeboys, Laurence de | Burwell | *ob* 1542 | 15 |
| Wardysworth, William | Betchworth | 1533 | 43 |
| Wenslagh, Simon de | Wensley | *c* 1360 | 81 |
| West, John | Sudborough | 1415 | 45 |
| White, John | Winchester College | *c* 1548 | 59 |
| Yong, John | Oxford (New College) | *ob* 1526 | 9 |

# INDEX OF PLACES

|  |  |  | FIG |
|---|---|---|---|
| Arundel | John Baker | 1445 | 33 |
| ,, | Esperaunce Blondell | c. 1450 | 34 |
| ,, | Adam Ertham | 1382 | 73 |
| Ashridge House | John de Swynstede | 1395 | 29 |
|  |  |  |  |
| Beachamwell | Thomas Chervyll (?) | c. 1380 | 27 |
| Beeford | Thomas Tonge | 1472 | 55 |
| Betchworth | William Wardysworth | 1533 | 43 |
| Bristol (Temple Church) | Anon | c. 1460 | 64 |
| Broadwater | John Mapilton | 1432 | 53 |
| Burwell | Laurence de Wardeboys | ob. 1542 | 15 |
| Byfleet | Thomas Teylar | c. 1480 | 66 |
|  |  |  |  |
| Cambridge (King's College) | Robert Hacombleyn | 1528 | 70 |
| Canterbury (St. George's) | John Lovelle | 1438 | 62 |
| Carlisle Cathedral | Richard Bell | 1496 | 8 |
| Carshalton | Walter Gaynesford | 1493 | 38 |
| Castle Ashby | William Ermyn | 1401 | 49 |
| Chigwell | Samuel Harsnett | 1631 | 4 |
| Cobham (Kent) | William Tanner | 1418 | 65 |
| Corringham | Richard de Beltoun | c. 1340 | 23 |
| Cottingham | Nicholas of Louth | 1383 | 74 |
| Croydon | Gabriel Silvester | 1512 | 57 |
| Dorchester (Oxon.) | Richard Bewfforeste | c. 1510 | 75 |
| Dronfield | Thomas Gomfrey | 1399 | 30 |
|  |  |  |  |
| East Horsley | John Bowthe | 1478 | 7 |
| East Malling | Richard Adams | 1522 | 69 |
| Ely Cathedral | Thomas Goodryke | 1554 | 10 |
| Eton College | Roger Lupton | 1540 | 79 |
| Exeter Cathedral | William Langeton | 1413 | 51 |
|  |  |  |  |
| Fulbourn | Anon. | c. 1390 | 28 |
| ,, | Geoffrey Byschop | 1477 | 37 |
|  |  |  |  |
| Great Bromley | William Byschopton | 1432 | 32 |
|  |  |  |  |
| Havant | Thomas Aileward | 1413 | 50 |
| Hereford Cathedral | John Trilleck | 1360 | 5 |

## The Ornaments of the Ministers, Etc.

|  |  |  | Fig |
|---|---|---|---|
| Higham Ferrars | Laurence St. Maur | 1337 | 21 |
| ,, ,, | St. Stephen | 1337 | 77 |
| Horsemonden | Henry de Grofhurst | c. 1340 | 22 |
| Horsham | Thomas Clerke | c 1411 | 44 |
| | | | |
| Kemsing | Thomas de Hop | c. 1320 | 18 |
| Knebworth | Simon Bache | 1414 | 52 |
| | | | |
| Laindon | Anon | c. 1470 | 36 |
| Lingfield | John Swetecok | 1469 | 35 |
| ,, | John Knoyll | 1503 | 39 |
| Littlebury | Anon. | c. 1510 | 41 |
| Little Easton | Robert Fyn | c. 1420 | 31 |
| | | | |
| Northfleet | Peter de Lacy | 1375 | 25 |
| Northleach | William Lawnder | c. 1530 | 76 |
| North Mimms | Thomas de Horton (?) | c 1360 | 82 |
| ,, Stoke | Roger Parkers | c. 1370 | 78 |
| | | | |
| Oulton (formerly at) | Adam de Bacon | c. 1310 | 16 |
| Oxford, Christ Church | James Coorthopp | 1557 | 71 |
| ,, Magdalen College | Arthur Cole | 1558 | 80 |
| ,, Merton ,, | Richard de Hakebourne | c. 1311 | 17 |
| ,, New ,, | Thomas Cranley | 1417 | 3 |
| ,, ,, ,, | John Yong | ob 1526 | 9 |
| ,, ,, ,, | John Frye | 1507 | 40 |
| ,, Queen's ,, | Robert Langton | 1518 | 58 |
| ,, ,, ,, | Henry Robinson | 1616 | 13 |
| | | | |
| Rochester (St. Margaret's) | Thomas Cod | 1465 | 60 |
| Rothwell | William de Rothewelle | c. 1361 | 46 |
| | | | |
| St Albans Abbey | Thomas Delamare | c 1375 | 83 |
| Salisbury Cathedral | Edmund Geste | 1578 | 11 |
| Shillington | Matthew de Asscheton | 1400 | 48 |
| Shottesbrooke | Anon. | c. 1370 | 24 |
| Stifford | Ralph Perchehay | 1378 | 26 |
| Stoke-in-Teignhead | Anon. | c 1320 | 19 |
| Sudborough | John West | 1415 | 45 |
| | | | |
| Tattershall | John Gyger (?) | c 1510 | 56 |
| Theydon Gernon | William Kirkeby | 1458 | 63 |
| Tideswell | Robert Pursglove | 1579 | 12 |
| Tong | Ralph Elcok | 1510 | 68 |
| | | | |
| Warbleton | William Prestwyk | 1436 | 54 |
| Watton | Anon. | c. 1370 | 72 |
| Wensley | Simon de Wenslagh | c. 1360 | 81 |

## The Ornaments of the Ministers, Etc.

|  |  |  | Fig |
|---|---|---|---|
| Westminster Abbey | Robert de Waldeby | 1397 | 2 |
| ,,      ,, | John de Waltham | 1395 | 6 |
| ,,      ,, | John Estney | 1498 | 14 |
| Winchester College | Edward Tacham | 1473 | 61 |
| ,,      ,, | John Gylbert | 1514 | 42 |
| ,,      ,, | John White | c. 1548 | 59 |
| ,,   St. Cross | John de Campeden | 1382 | 47 |
| ,,      ,, | Richard Harward | 1493 | 67 |
| Woodchurch | Nichol de Gore | c. 1330 | 20 |
| York Minster | William de Grenefeld | 1315 | 1 |

# INDEX OF DATES

|  |  |  | FIG |
|---|---|---|---|
| c. 1310 | Adam de Bacon | Oulton (formerly at) | 16 |
| c. 1311 | Richard de Hakebourne | Oxford (Merton College) | 17 |
| 1315 | William de Grenefeld | York Minster | 1 |
| c 1320 | Thomas de Hop | Kemsing | 18 |
| c 1320 | Anon | Stoke-in-Teignhead | 19 |
| c. 1330 | Nichol de Gore | Woodchurch | 20 |
| 1337 | Laurence St. Maur | Higham Ferrars | 21 |
| 1337 | St. Stephen | Higham Ferrars | 77 |
| c. 1340 | Henry de Grofhurst | Horsemonden | 22 |
| c. 1340 | Richard de Beltoun | Corringham | 23 |
| c. 1360 | Simon de Wenslagh | Wensley | 81 |
| c. 1360 | Thomas de Horton (?) | North Mimms | 82 |
| 1360 | John Trilleck | Hereford Cathedral | 5 |
| c 1361 | William de Rothewelle | Rothwell | 46 |
| c. 1370 | Roger Parkers | North Stoke | 78 |
| c. 1370 | Anon. | Shottesbrooke | 24 |
| c 1370 | Anon | Watton | 72 |
| 1375 | Peter de Lacy | Northfleet | 25 |
| c. 1375 | Thomas Delamare | St. Albans Abbey | 83 |
| 1378 | Ralph Perchehay | Stifford | 26 |
| c 1380 | Thomas Chervyll (?) | Beachamwell | 27 |
| 1382 | John de Campeden | Winchester (St. Cross) | 47 |
| 1382 | Adam Ertham | Arundel | 73 |
| 1383 | Nicholas of Louth | Cottingham | 74 |
| c. 1390 | Anon. | Fulbourn | 28 |
| 1395 | John de Swynstede | Ashridge House | 29 |
| 1395 | John de Waltham | Westminster Abbey | 6 |
| 1397 | Robert de Waldeby | Westminster Abbey | 2 |
| 1399 | Thomas Gomfrey | Dronfield | 30 |
| 1400 | Matthew de Asscheton | Shillington | 48 |
| 1401 | William Ermyn | Castle Ashby | 49 |
| c. 1411 | Thomas Clerke | Horsham | 44 |
| 1413 | Thomas Aileward | Havant | 50 |
| 1413 | William Langeton | Exeter Cathedral | 51 |
| 1414 | Simon Bache | Knebworth | 52 |
| 1415 | John West | Sudborough | 45 |
| 1417 | Thomas Cranley | Oxford (New College) | 3 |
| 1418 | William Tanner | Cobham (Kent) | 65 |
| c 1420 | Robert Fyn | Little Easton | 31 |
| 1432 | William Byschopton | Great Bromley | 32 |
| 1432 | John Mapilton | Broadwater | 53 |
| 1436 | William Prestwyk | Warbleton | 54 |

189

# The Ornaments of the Ministers, Etc.

|  |  |  | FIG |
|---|---|---|---|
| 1438 | John Lovelle | Canterbury (St. George's) | 62 |
| 1445 | John Baker | Arundel | 33 |
| c. 1450 | Esperaunce Blondell | Arundel | 34 |
| 1458 | William Kirkeby | Theydon Gernon | 63 |
| c. 1460 | Anon. | Bristol (Temple Church) | 64 |
| 1465 | Thomas Cod | Rochester (St. Margaret's) | 60 |
| 1469 | John Swetecok | Lingfield | 35 |
| c. 1470 | Anon. | Laindon | 36 |
| 1472 | Thomas Tonge | Beeford | 55 |
| 1473 | Edward Tacham | Winchester College | 61 |
| 1477 | Geoffrey Byschop | Fulbourn | 37 |
| 1478 | John Bowthe | East Horsley | 7 |
| c. 1480 | Thomas Teylar | Byfleet | 66 |
| 1493 | Walter Gaynesford | Carshalton | 38 |
| 1493 | Richard Harward | Winchester (St. Cross) | 67 |
| 1496 | Richard Bell | Carlisle Cathedral | 8 |
| 1498 | John Estney | Westminster Abbey | 14 |
| 1503 | John Knoyll | Lingfield | 39 |
| 1507 | John Frye | Oxford (New College) | 40 |
| c. 1510 | Anon. | Littlebury | 41 |
| c. 1510 | John Gyger (?) | Tattershall | 56 |
| c. 1510 | Richard Bewfforeste | Dorchester (Oxon.) | 75 |
| 1510 | Ralph Elcok | Tong | 68 |
| 1512 | Gabriel Silvester | Croydon | 57 |
| 1514 | John Gylbert | Winchester College | 42 |
| 1518 | Robert Langton | Oxford (Queen's College) | 58 |
| 1522 | Richard Adams | East Malling | 69 |
| ob. 1526 | John Yong | Oxford (New College) | 9 |
| 1528 | Robert Hacombleyn | Cambridge (King's College) | 70 |
| c. 1530 | William Lawnder | Northleach | 76 |
| 1533 | William Wardysworth | Betchworth | 43 |
| 1540 | Roger Lupton | Eton College | 79 |
| ob. 1542 | Laurence de Wardeboys | Burwell | 15 |
| c. 1548 | John White | Winchester College | 59 |
| 1554 | Thomas Goodryke | Ely Cathedral | 10 |
| 1557 | James Coorthopp | Oxford (Christ Church) | 71 |
| 1558 | Arthur Cole | Oxford (Magdalen College) | 80 |
| 1578 | Edmund Geste | Salisbury Cathedral | 11 |
| 1579 | Robert Pursglove | Tideswell | 12 |
| 1616 | Henry Robinson | Oxford (Queen's College) | 13 |
| 1631 | Samuel Harsnett | Chigwell | 4 |

www.ingramcontent.com/pod-product-compliance
Lightning Source LLC
Chambersburg PA
CBHW072131160426
43197CB00012B/2066